Fulfilled.

52 Prescriptions for Healing, Health, and Happiness

BERNADETTE ANDERSON, M.D., M.P.H.

FOREWORD BY HOWARD MURAD, M.D.

Fulfilled

52 Prescriptions for
Healing, Health, and Happiness

DR. BERNADETTE ANDERSON
FOREWORD BY HOWARD MURAD, M.D.

woodhall press

Woodhall Press | Norwalk, CT

woodhall press

Woodhall Press, 81 Old Saugatuck Road, Norwalk, CT 06855
WoodhallPress.com

Cover design: Asha Hossain
Layout artist: LJ Mucci

Library of Congress Cataloging-in-Publication Data available
ISBN 978-1-954907-23-2   (paper: alk paper)
ISBN 978-1-954907-24-9   (electronic)

First Edition
Distributed by Independent Publishers Group
(800) 888-4741

Printed in the United States of America

Disclaimer

The publisher and the author are providing this book and its contents on an "as is" basis and make no representations or warranties of any kind with respect to this book or its contents. The publisher and the author disclaim all such representations and warranties, including but not limited to warranties of healthcare for a particular purpose. In addition, the publisher and the author assume no responsibility for errors, inaccuracies, omissions, or any other inconsistencies herein.

The content of this book is for informational purposes only and is not intended to diagnose, treat, cure, or prevent any condition or disease. You understand that this book is not intended as a substitute for consultation with a licensed practitioner. Please consult with your own physician or healthcare specialist regarding the suggestions and recommendations made in this book. The use of this book implies your acceptance of this disclaimer.

The publisher and the author make no guarantees concerning the level of success you may experience by following the advice and strategies contained in this book, and you accept the risk that results will differ for each individual. The testimonials and examples provided in this book show exceptional results, which may not apply to the average reader, and are not intended to represent or guarantee that you will achieve the same or similar results.

Especially to You,
(yes, you)

Life throws curve balls that leave you breathless. It took me many months to stop privately crying long enough to exhale and find my way. We are often waiting for permission to be vulnerable and let go, not realizing it comes from within. Life is a complex journey, but at least now you have a manual. And I'll know if you read it. Because I have walked more than my share of miles in uncomfortable shoes, maybe a pair similar to yours.

The Prescriptions in this book are not intended to replace medical advice from a qualified health provider and should not be used as such. They are meant to increase awareness and insight and guide you in taking action to become who you were born to be—and nothing less. Consult your physician or health provider to determine the appropriateness of the information for you and to diagnosis and treat health conditions.

PROLOGUE

The sole intention of this prologue is to get you to read this book. Nothing more, nothing less.

Let's be honest, who wants to drudge through the hard stuff? I didn't. I am still not a fan of the process. But here is the thing, there is no way around it other than denial. And that likely won't end well. I tried it. Now I am the author of a self-help book, so go figure. My life lessons are sprawled over these pages so you can live full of purpose too.

It wasn't romance that swept me off my feet. It was heartaches, challenges, and unpleasant experiences that caused me to lose my footing. I staggered in circles, tripping over life until it was crystal clear that I couldn't escape the parts of my story I didn't like. I had to heal from them. That may not have been what you wanted to read. Perhaps you were wishing the ugly parts of your story would simply go away. They likely won't. Not without *you* aligning the sun, the moon, and the stars.

Life isn't smooth sailing, nor is that a realistic expectation. But the waters became less choppy when I acknowledged my father's neglect, admitted I was estranged from my own life, stopped using a fork to do my heavy lifting. And I released the pain of not being a biological mother. It was as if I had taken the breath necessary for my heart to beat again. Your turn.

I said it earlier; I want you to read this book. I also want you to be engaged. Why? The obvious reason is that I've poured my soul and energy into it. But more so because, in some shape or form, healing, health, and happiness are on everyone's wish list. Well, health and happiness are, but they lie in wait of healing. This book is your action plan to create the life you daydream about, the one that makes every fiber of your being leap, be the one that you live!

CONTENTS

HEALTH

HAPPINESS

FOREWORD

by Dr. Howard Murad

A beautiful, sincere thank-you note inspired me to extend Dr. Bernadette an invitation to my inaugural Inclusive Health Wellness Retreat. It was there I had the pleasure of personally interacting with Dr. B. That initial connection is all it took. It was the spark on which to build a professional relationship and a dear friendship. Since our first meeting, we've created a health and wellness video series, partnered on articles, and even enjoyed some karaoke! Our visits are always invigorating for the soul, and a downright good time.

As the "Father of Modern Wellness" and founder of Murad Skincare, I share similar philosophies with Dr. B. That is, we wholly believe in curating a lifestyle that supports living a healthier, happier, and more fulfilling life. It is no surprise to me that she wrote this heartfelt and well-crafted guide, *Fulfilled. 52 Prescriptions for Healing, Health, and Happiness,* to provide everyone with a clear road map to find the best version of ourselves! If anyone can point us in the right direction, it's Dr. B. She is brimming with passion, intellect, and commitment in terms of broadening our collective scope of what it means to live healthily physically, mentally, and spiritually. You need only spend a few moments with her—or read a few chapters of this book—to feel the deep intention of her mission.

My own research confirms the importance of reconnecting with what makes you *happy.* A happy place is one we all strive to occupy, and Dr. B—through this book—gives us the compass to find and live in this space by figuring out and letting go of whatever limiting beliefs block our happiness. I've observed her illustrate this in her fun nature and joyous, contagious laughter.

This guide and its Prescriptions are a valuable resource and investment. The wealth of information it contains enlightens, equips, and empowers you to fully awaken to your ideal life. Enjoy your journey with Dr. B—it will be a life-changer! She believes in you.

A QUICK GUIDE FOR USING THIS BOOK

Step 1: Prepare

This book is not designed to be a passive read. Healing, restoring your health, and enjoying happiness require some work on your part, but this book ensures that you have the right road map for success.

Expect the words and Prescriptions within this book to propel you into action. Let them serve as your compass to stay on track and create the life you rightfully deserve. Throughout these pages, I share lessons from my own struggles and experiences because it is my way of holding your hand and encouraging you as you begin your life-changing journey!

Aim to set aside time when you will be least distracted and when you can freely lean into the process, giving each topic the attention needed in order to show up as your best self in that particular area.

Along with this book, there are a few other things I suggest you have on hand:

1. Three journals or notebooks for extra space to organize your notes and room to explore your thoughts. Why? As you grow from each baby step, you may decide to add more to what you've previously written.

2. Keep a special pen or pencil nearby to be used only for this book and the journal. This is a small gesture that makes it feel especially yours.

3. Lastly, be ready to extend yourself loads of self-compassion and grace.

52 Guides and Prescriptions

This book contains 52 guides accompanied with Prescriptions. I refer to them as "Prescriptions" because they are a catalyst for healing, health, and happiness. Although this book is organized into 52 weekly guides, covering the span of a year, you can set your own pace to pursue what is possible for your life. *You* decide how to incorporate them into *your* schedule—daily, three times a week, or weekly. Staying committed to achieving the life you deserve is the priority.

Everyone is a work in progress—including me. Find comfort in knowing that I have applied these same principles to my life, and they have worked. As with most things, you will only get out of it what you put into it.

There is no set order
Yes, you read that correctly: There is no set order in which to approach the readings. That said, they are grouped into sections—Healing, Health, and Happiness. It works best when you complete an entire section before moving on to the next, but it really is your choice. To begin your journey, I recommend starting with and working through "Healing." While it may be a bit more challenging than the other sections, there is something to be said about experiencing health and happiness with a healed soul. But we are all at different places, so start this book wherever it feels right for you.

What's important is that you use this book often and engage in the process. If you remain dedicated, it will be an influential navigation tool for revealing your best life.

What to expect
The time we spend together here is meant to support you in switching gears from dreaming to actually making your best life happen. We will tap into your authentic self to uncover what may be preventing the real you from emerging as well as identify any obstacles in the way of your ambitions. The goal is to restore your hope and discover a safe mental place where you can heal and become intentional—being at one with your actions and your purpose—about living a healthy, happy life.

Step 2: Decide you are worth it

Becoming unstuck and gathering the courage to live a fulfilling life requires rolling up your sleeves and putting muscle into shifting your life in the direction of your choice. Yes, it will require some time, sweat, and possibly a few tears, but you are the only one who can decide to do the work necessary to manifest the outcome you want for your life.

Trust me when I say that you already have the ability within you to live out your most meaningful life. Now, just decide if you're worth it and if you're ready.

Are you worth it? YES

Before you move forward, before you attempt to embark on a transformational journey, you must *believe you are worth it*. If you don't, it will be more difficult to get the most out of this book. Self-worth greatly influences your behaviors and thoughts. It empowers you to take action instead of passively waiting for something to happen. Life isn't happening to you—you are molding it, and you must determine whether you will be an active participant or a passive one.

If you are not yet there, perhaps taking a step back to build self-worth and believe in yourself again is the first step you need before starting this journey. I want to set you up for success by influencing you to be intentional in eliminating self-criticism through self-compassion, change the narrative of your story so you are no longer the victim, and define what makes you valuable.

Committing

If you have made up your mind that you are ready to make your vision your reality, and you have concluded that you *are* worth it, then the next step is commitment. I wish I could tell you the life you seek will occur overnight, but that's not the reality. Instead, embrace time. Permit yourself to take as long as you need. You are worth the time.

Step 3: Set and protect your boundaries

Embracing and maintaining boundaries are the truest measures of self-respect. I am guilty. I've set boundaries but failed to protect them. I'm not alone in this struggle, because it's a tough one. But why? Is it self-sabotage, fear, not wanting to take ownership—all of the above? Boundaries are a way to become very clear about yourself. And when you have clarity, you become the captain of your own ship and can determine the course you'll take.

For the purpose of this book, boundaries will help you stay on track and do the hard yards. They'll serve you in aligning yourself for genuine happiness and empower you to release the outcomes.

Measurement for Success

Nina Shadi's story of the lotus flower, from The Awakened Heart Project, is a perfect depiction of the pathway, strength, and big change I want you to experience as you work through each Prescription. In her words:

> The lotus begins its journey under water surrounded by mud and muck, by fish and insects, and in dirty, rough environments. The lotus flower maintains strength and pushes aside each dirty obstacle as it makes its way to clearer surfaces. At this time, the lotus is still just a stem with only a few leaves, and a small flower pod. But in time, the stem continues to grow, and the pod slowly surfaces above the water into the clean air, finally freeing itself from the harsh conditions below. It is then when the lotus slowly opens each beautiful petal to the sun, basking in the surrounding worldly beauty. The lotus flower is ready to take on the world.
>
> Despite being born into dark, murky conditions, where hope for such beautiful life seems dubious, the lotus grows and rises above adversity. Ironically, this same dirty water washes it clean as it surfaces. As the lotus opens each petal to the air, not a stain or spot of mud remains externally. The inner lotus, too, has never seen a drop of mud or dirty water. It is pure, bright, and beautiful.

Lotus Levels
Some of the Prescriptions are easier than others, so I created a set of visuals to let you know what to expect as you begin

each one. This way, you can plan, prepare, or pause to determine whether to forge ahead or come back when it's better
for you. I call them "Lotus Levels." They denote how much
emotional or mental work you may need to invest to complete
the Prescription. Keep in mind, this is a subjective measure-
ment. Everyone is approaching this guide from a different
place on their journey. No two approaches are the same, and
no approach is wrong.

There are four Lotus Levels: Level 1 represents light effort,
while Level 4 requires a greater emotional and mental under-
taking to get maximum results. When the Lotus Level increases,
don't lose heart. Remember, you are worth it! Your hard work
will lead to many personal rewards.

Lotus Level 1: Open Your Petals

This level involves light effort and is intended to give you a
break to come up for air.

Recommended Environment: A quiet, but not necessarily
private, setting is ideal.

Lotus Level 2: Take Deep Breaths

This level is where you are growing and blossoming. It requires
a bit more personal insight than Lotus Level 1.

Recommended Environment: It's your choice to work in
private or not.

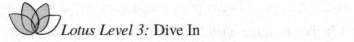*Lotus Level 3:* Dive In

This level is where you gather the strength to push aside obstacles. It's more intense than the first two.

Recommended Environment: In private.

Lotus Level 4: Explore the Root

This level is where the work may feel the most arduous. You're searching for the light to gain clarity, persevere, and survive whatever you've been through.

Recommended Environment: Close the door. This is a private affair.

Definitions: The Bits-n-Bobs of This Book

Prescriptions

At the end of each chapter there is a Prescription that relates to the topic. This is when you apply the readings to your own life and make it about you.

Although it may be tempting, do not skip the Prescriptions. They are the portal for real and lasting transformation. I encourage you to give them plenty of thought and reflection.

Journal Pages

At the back of the book are blank, lined pages. Use them as you please. On these pages you can go into more detail about your answers to the Prescription questions, express any feelings you are having, pose additional questions to yourself, or doodle to process it all. It's extra room for you to delve a little deeper and release your mind.

Record Your Triumphs

There are times when it may feel as though no matter how hard you try, you are not making progress, especially when it comes to shifting your life in a positive direction. That's why you must keep a list of your triumphs. Record your achievements in the designated section at the back of the book. What a great reminder of your accomplishments! I began doing this when a friend compiled a list of my business successes over a year and shared them with me. I was floored by all I had done and got to relive that feeling of accomplishment. Remembering your breakthroughs will boost your self-esteem and keep you feeling encouraged.

Getting Started:
Move Slowly and with Intention

Are you ready for the life you deserve?
Read that question a few times and let it sink in. Slow down. Take a breath. Be still with your thoughts—this is a powerful moment.

You've already taken an important step forward by opening this book, but saying yes to that question (and meaning it) is what will shape your experience and put you on a path to self-revelation. Do be careful of intuitively responding "yes" because it seems like the answer you are expected to give. No one is watching or judging you.

If you approach this book by being honest with yourself, you have the sensational freedom to learn about your *true self*. And as your honesty meets your willingness to change, you open yourself up to pursue your passion and purpose. Being genuine is the only way to receive the most rewards for your investment in this book and its Prescriptions.

Breathe
This is a good time to take a deep breath—I'll share more about breathwork later—and get your life's vision in front of you. You have put the life you were born to live on hold for far too long. Here and now is your season to go for it—deliberately live the life you deserve from this point on! Take this

moment to . . . breathe in. Hold the breath. Release it slowly. Repeat the cycle once more.

> **It is not the mountain we conquer but ourselves.**
>
> **—Sir Edmund Hillary**

"

Be calm,
breathe,
and

think.

—My niece Aubrey Denise Elaine Rowe
(at only 4 years old)

"

Healing

1

A POSITIVE MINDSET MATTERS

- Do you look for the silver lining in tough times?

- What are you grateful for right now?

You cannot tailor-make the situations in life, but you can tailor-make the attitudes to fit those situations.

—Zig Ziglar

Negative thoughts have a way of sliding into our thinking. They prick and prod our emotions until we're left lying face-down on the floor, unable to muster the energy to head them off. The downward spiral into gloom and doom becomes faster, faster, and faster as we desperately attempt to brace ourselves to avoid being devoured by cynicism and falling into a slump. We're all vulnerable. I admit it's a familiar scenario to me. One bad seed planted in our minds can quickly grow into a garden of pessimism.

The truth is, life *is* going to trip us up from time to time—count on it. But if we refuse to retreat to a negative frame of mind, the sun will rise again—our harvest season will return.

My father drove past me

I know just how it feels to try to stay upbeat and hit it out of the park when life isn't playing fair. Much like it felt the times when I watched my father drive past me to drop his step-daughter off at school with no concern about how I got there. To be fully transparent, I didn't exactly bubble up inside and have a full-on positivity movement—then and not now. My father's thoughtlessness made me feel bad. But I learned to cope with (not deny) the disappointment. Eventually, consciously or subconsciously, the school drop-offs catapulted my studies into a full scholarship to attend the University of Michigan.

Flat out refuse to grant your mind permission to bully you. Positivity is your most prized possession. It's your golden ticket to withstand the headwinds of negativity—without it, you'll likely fall victim to the situation.

The power of positivity

Is nothing working out? Or is it not working out exactly like you planned? There's a difference. You've heard that "the power of positivity is immense." It is a popular sentiment echoed by great leaders and inspirational speakers worldwide. It's true. There is boundless proof affirming that both your mindset and perspective have a remarkable and direct influence on the life you live. Having a positive attitude is the difference between attracting what you want, settling for what you get, or allowing your journey to totally devastate you.

What is a positive mindset?

No one has full immunity against negativity—there will be times when you need to cry, and you should. But some people certainly seem to be hard-wired with more positive DNA than others. Regardless, cultivating a positive mindset can be done by anyone who approaches it with conscious intention. It is a way of embracing life so that even when negative messages spring up—and they will—you don't believe them. They don't form a hostile mental takeover, and you can trust that "all's well that ends well."

When you continue to reach for the positive version of you, it invites life's sweet melody to play in your life and silences the harsh background noises. Some days are harder than others—that's real life. Those times require being genuinely authentic to your soul to break through mental barriers.

You can shift gears

Thinking with a positive mind ignites a spark that can entirely change the way you live your life. For me, a positive outlook, positive self-talk, and positive actions shifted my attention to how things *can* happen instead of what cannot happen. Yes, obstacles show up, but they only get in the way if you let them.

I am the daughter of a single mother, and some people may view that as being a negative experience. Admittedly, it wasn't always easy, but so many of my strengths—the ones that led to my becoming a doctor and author—blossomed from it. I learned to make the most of the cards I was dealt in life. It turned out to be my royal flush—my best possible hand! How can you apply that way of thinking in your life?

The blessings in disguise

Optimism is the launchpad for attracting goodness, grace, and fulfillment in your life. It lands you in the driver's seat and allows you to steer life in the direction you choose. You have much more control over what materializes—or doesn't—than you give yourself credit for.

Positivity renews the mind, body, and spirit. Being able to see the blessings in disguise expands your world because negativity won't blind you from something good just because it wasn't what you had hoped for. Celebrate the highs and learn from the lows; they both play a powerful role in bringing out the best in you.

We can complain
because the rose
bushes have thorns,
or rejoice because the
thorn bushes

have roses.

—Abraham Lincoln

PRESCRIPTION

For a Positive Mindset

1

Adopting a positive attitude doesn't mean pretending you never have valley experiences. When you focus on the brighter side, it lets you see those low, valley experiences as *temporary* conditions that provide you with an opportunity to call your strengths into play.

Twists and turns are significant to every journey. It's important to remember that all things—the good and the not-so-good—work together for your favor. The challenge is remaining in the right state of mind: a positive one. Now that we're on the same page, let's take the first step toward fostering positivity in your life!

The more aware you are of what unfavorably affects your positive mood or outlook, the better you can protect it. To begin your pursuit of optimism, identify five things (or people) that cause negative clouds to form in your life. Feel free to write them below, in the journal pages after this section, or on a separate piece of paper.

1.

2.

3.

4.

5.

Next, answer the following questions for each of the five things or persons you identified:

a. Why does this person or situation arouse negative emotions?

b. Have you contributed to the negative undercurrent? If so, how?

c. What can you do to lessen the unpleasant effects of this thing or person in your life?

d. What are at least three positives about the event or situation with each person? Dig deep.

e. How can you be intentional (align actions with purpose) about changing your negative reactions toward it or the person?

Follow-up steps:

1. Take a few minutes to identify some negative thoughts you play over and over in your mind, like a broken record.

2. Write a few down, then reword them as affirmations instead of negative statements. For example, instead of "I hate my body," state: "I want to become healthier and more fit."

3. Each time the familiar negative recording starts to play, pause it and replace it with a new, positive one. Dog-ear this page and visit this section frequently to process negative thoughts.

Life is not always going to smell like a rose, but your perception can prevent a bad smell or undesirable circumstance from lingering. Do not be deterred by setbacks; instead, take an alternative point of view, a deeper look inward, and let obstacles inspire you to evolve into the best version of yourself.

I'll end Prescription 1 on this note: You cannot change what has happened, but training your mind to think positively profoundly changes its impact on your life.

Time to celebrate!

You took the first step on your journey to a more joyful and fulfilling life. Celebrate! If you have had specific victories, record them in the Triumph section located in the back of the book. Make affirmations, recognition, and rewards a habit. This is a good time to pick up a couple of journals or create your own.

SCIENCE SAYS...

"Optimists are 5 times
less likely than pessimists
to get burned out."

—S. Achor and M. Gielan, Optimism Scale

YOU WERE
BORN WHOLE

- What's stopping you from feeling complete within yourself?

- How can you feel more confident that you're enough?

You, alone, make a whole person.

—Christine Caine

When I look at my niece, I can hardly believe this small child has everything she needs to mature into the unique person she was created to be. She doesn't have to wait for someone or something to complete her—she was born whole. We are *all* born whole. People and things can only complement our whole self. We are not in a holding pattern because something *is* missing, but because we haven't discerned that whatever we believe is missing *has been present* all along. When we recognize we are not on standby, we become free and open to live a full life.

What does it mean to be whole?

You aren't a jigsaw puzzle, nor have you fallen off the wall and are waiting to be put back together again. And, in case you were wondering, you are not one half of a person in pursuit of your better half to complete you.

Living whole starts with believing you are *not* incomplete and to know undoubtedly that you are enough. Wholeness is living in harmony in mind, body, and spirit while purposefully nurturing all aspects of your being. You are available to live your whole experience—you can see the forest *and* the trees. You're open to permitting your life to unfold without forcing it to be anything other than what it was meant to be because you are secure about who you are personally and spiritually, and why you are here.

Wholeness is the peace that surpasses all understanding. It means you . . .

- acknowledge and are honest about your real feelings.

- are receptive and don't take things personally when they are not personal.
- reserve your energy for what supports your life.
- design a life that is less crowed and less complicated.
- embrace all three dimensions of yourself—mind, body, and spirit.
- feel at home within yourself.
- invite healing—with open arms—into your broken places.

Wholeness is not effortless

Encountering brokenness does not condemn you to a lifetime of hopelessness—although it may feel that way when you're in the midst of it—nor should it destroy your self-worth. The truth is, you'll face situations that leave you standing on the corner of brokenness and despair, picking up the shattered pieces of your life. At some point, we all find ourselves roaming that street. Ironically, those valley moments can bear good fruit: renewed or newfound faith, increased strength, and solid trust. And consider this: A whole egg comes out of a broken shell, so wholeness can come from brokenness.

Living whole is by no means effortless. It is a mindful journey or, better yet, a lifestyle from which you grow beyond bad decisions instead of shrinking into their shadows.

So, how do you live whole?

You came into this world as a whole person, and it is possible that life experiences and traumas caused you to lose touch with your sense of being complete. Let's help you return to your whole self.

The key is to accept you in your entirety and not just the fraction of you that everyone—including yourself—knows and adores. Become acquainted with the parts of you that you've shunned. There are no aspects of you that are shameful or unworthy. So there's no reason to try to cover up what the world may see as a flaw or blemish, because they're an important part of the whole you. Going further, address what made you feel broken in the first place. This is no small feat, but it's very necessary in order to put the fragmented pieces of you back together again and stop living as damaged goods. There was a time I thought I'd be complete once I was married, had children, and achieved my goals. When those things didn't play out the way I had imagined they would, my broken heart wept silently and inconsolably. Little did I know, those milestones didn't authenticate my wholeness. I always was and always will be a whole person. And that holds true for you too.

Now that you know what to do, how do you do it? Love yourself unconditionally—without the need to be perfect. Be careful of compromising the whole you to live up to an outward appearance. Allow yourself to continuously discover your truth and admit there are areas where you feel incomplete; it's the only way to heal and fill the emptiness.

When you strive for harmony within yourself, you'll find you attract the things that make you feel whole. Step into the whole you, gift yourself more love, listen to the wisdom of the soul, and claim the life you were meant to live.

Breathe in this new perspective

Let's take a moment to pause and breathe into this concept, because learning to be honest with yourself and live wholly is a huge deal. You may even need to reclaim the pieces of yourself that you gave away. That's okay. For now, take a breath. Breathe in through your nose. Hold it for a moment. Release your breath slowly from your mouth. If it feels good, repeat the cycle a few times—the power of the breath is restorative.

> When your body, mind, and soul are healthy and harmonious, you will bring health and harmony to the world—not by withdrawing from the world, but by being a healthy, living organ of the body of humanity.
>
> **—Christine Caine**

PRESCRIPTION

For Living Your Life Whole

You are not a part of a whole—you *are* whole. In my personal experience, wholeness is the art of loving the *whole you* in order to gain access to your most meaningful life. And you are the only one who has the capacity to restore wholeness—to reintegrate the broken pieces—in your life. Are you ready to live life on a *whole* new level? Yes!

Use the following 12-Step Plan to process what has you feeling all broken up, including what makes you feel flawed or not enough.

12-Step Plan to Living Your Whole Life

1. Dismiss self-judgment; it serves no purpose. Develop a habit of appreciativeness. What are the things you most appreciate about yourself? List them.

2. Embrace imperfections; they are a part of what perfects you. Write down three to five self-perceived inadequacies, and beside each state how you could play them to your strengths. This step makes me think of a friend who suffered an eye condition. His recovery required him to keep his head facing down. This was frustrating until he dug out art supplies he had previously purchased (with no intention of actually using) from a retreat and started painting. He used his restrictions to create art—hundreds of pieces of art—some of which have been sold in charity auctions.

3. Address self-limiting beliefs. What are you allowing to hold you back? Write them on a piece of paper, then throw it away. It frees up the energy you lose when denying your selfhood.

4. Master being *you*. What are your likes and dislikes, your secret pleasures, your rather-nots? Get to know yourself by writing your real-world story. Not the safe public-facing one, but the personal story you were born to share.

5. Change where you are searching. You're fully equipped to be you, which means the answers are within—you have everything you need right now. Ask yourself why you're trying to redirect your life in a direction other than the one you're destined to travel.

6. Investigate thoughts that make you feel inadequate. Where are they stemming from, and why won't you let them go?

7. Love yourself at all times, despite your choices. More is coming later in the book, because I realize this is not always easy work. Start simply by developing a habit of telling yourself something positive about yourself every day. Give it a try right now.

8. Let bygones be bygones. They're mere distractions from the here and now. What do you need to focus on to get closer to your desired destination?

9. Be guided by your own heart and intuitions. Become familiar with the voice of your own soul. Practice sitting in stillness, closing your eyes, and hearing the subtle tone and sound of your inner voice directing your journey. Practice this more than once, because forming a good habit takes time. It'll become louder, clearer, less fearful, and reliable each time.

10. Grow from "it." How can you repurpose what may have been meant to harm you into something that will help you achieve your real purpose? Recall a challenging experience. What are some positive lessons you can take from it?

11. Nurture your mind, body, and spirit—stop here and do this three-minute exercise.

    a. Sit comfortably, close your eyes, and be aware of your experience—sounds, smells, sensations, and thoughts—without trying to change them.

    b. Take full, deep breaths: in through your nose and out through your mouth.

c. With each inhalation and exhalation, notice the sensation of your breath and allow your body to become more relaxed.

d. Repeat for eight cycles.

e. Bring your awareness back to the room. Open your eyes.

12. First, be true to you—keeping up appearances is exhausting. What blemishes are you trying to cover up? They may be a source to connect as opposed to a drawback that turns people away.

"

Wholeness will
empower you to
shatter every barrier
that keeps you
from the winning
opportunities God has
in store for

you.

—Touré Roberts

"

LOVE WHO
YOU ARE

- What makes you beautifully unique?

- What does self-love look like to you on a daily basis?

> To be yourself in a world that
> is constantly trying to make
> you something else is the
> greatest accomplishment.
>
> **—Ralph Waldo Emerson**

I wish I looked like her.

I wish my hair and skin were like hers.

I wish I had his charm.

I wish I had his talent.

I wish I exuded their confidence.

Admittedly, I've quietly wished my appearance and aura were more like someone else's. It's human nature to want what you don't have—that's not to say you cannot recognize and acknowledge beauty in others. Quite the opposite! To acknowledge someone's beauty is a beautiful thing; however, comparing yourself to them is not. I had no idea how disrespectful I was being to myself when I devalued my own unique beauty, gifts, and abilities. At times, loving yourself is a love-hate relationship, but when you master self-love, every aspect of your life is radically transformed. And life happens on a whole other level; your world will go 'round.

Are you your inner critic?

I'll let you in on a little secret: Your eyes, cheekbones, smile, skin, hair, curves, muscles, legs, insight, mastery of words, skills, or talent has caught someone's eye. Yes, *you* have a lot to be admired. But what really matters is: Can you genuinely appreciate yourself, or are you your inner critic? Instead of criticizing what makes you beautifully different, channel that energy into loving who you are.

You are playing the leading role in your life. It's okay to desire to look and dress the part—pick up a new shade of lipstick, curl your lashes, hone in on your talents, invest in what makes you feel unstoppable. You should absolutely aim to be your best, *inside* and out. Just know that real makeovers are much more than skin-deep. They penetrate physical barriers to refine your core.

Love is hard but rewarding

It's exhausting to continually disassociate yourself from who you really are, and you miss out on a grand experience that can only be had by you. Love every appealing trait and perfect imperfection about you, the whole package. They all melodiously blend to create a fearfully and wonderfully made you!

Do away with the comparison game—it's self-defeating. If everyone looked and behaved the same, the world would be boring. Have the courage to accept your individual awesomeness. When you defy the social standards of beauty and behavior to define your own, you will live stronger and happier.

How do you learn to love yourself?

See your own beauty, including the beauty within! Find something about yourself to fall in love with—your quirky laugh, your kindness, your wisdom.

There was a time when I'd never get dressed in front of a mirror because I could only see everything that I wasn't. I wasn't thin. I wasn't tall. I wasn't shaped like a model—you know what I mean. Focusing on what I wasn't blinded me to seeing all that I *was*. I had to pull up the shade of the narrow, skin-deep image of beauty. What happened next? I exposed a uniquely tailored Me, suited for excellence and without need for alteration. I just needed to learn to love Her (Me) and treat Her as someone I loved.

Be ecstatic about who you are and what you exclusively contribute to the world. Tap into that energy to start unconditionally loving yourself more. Somewhere inside, your light has been flickering, trying to get your attention. Stoke that fire and let it shine! Refuse to let anyone or anything snuff it out.

Embrace imperfection

Love that you are perfectly imperfect.

Love that your beauty is like no other.

Love your essence.

Love your uniqueness.

Love your body.

Love your sense of humor.

Fall head over heels in love with *yourself*.

Listen to your own voice

For me, one of the most powerful things about loving who I am is being able to hear and listen to my voice over others'. It positions me to discredit unfounded opinions and comments.

Because ultimately, I have the final say, and only I know my truth. I encourage you to listen to your own voice and give it the clout it deserves. It's what you think of yourself that counts.

> Loving
> ourselves works
> miracles in our
> *lives.*

—**Louise Hay**

PRESCRIPTION 3

For Learning to Love Who You Are

Have you ever made a brag book for a child or someone you love? The name is self-explanatory, but the intent is to capture positivity. Take a few moments now to brag about yourself. No one is looking—there is no judgment—so toot your own horn as loud as you want! Remind yourself of your awesome features, talents, and qualities. Don't wait for a compliment; offer yourself one, now.

- Let's get visual! Who doesn't want to look at a beautiful photo of themselves? On one of the blank journal pages following this Prescription, tape a picture of yourself that you love and exudes positivity.

- Learn to give yourself a compliment. List three of your physical attributes that you adore.

a.

b.

c.

- How can you showcase these qualities more often? Be a show-off!

- Write down three of your talents—more if you really feel like bragging.

a.

b.

c.

- How can these gifts be routinely infused into your daily life?

- List five of your most amazing characteristics.
  a.
  b.
  c.
  d.
  e.

- How do your talents and skills enrich your life?

> We can climb
> mountains with
>
> *self-love.*
>
> —Samira Wiley

4 ACCEPT WHAT YOU CANNOT CHANGE

- What are you refusing to accept in your life?

- Do you spend a lot of time worrying about what you can't change?

> A moment of radical acceptance is a moment of genuine freedom.
>
> **—T. Brach**

In the past, the idea of acceptance did not sit well with me. Partially because I let my emotions get the better of me, and, to be honest, acceptance felt like a cop-out. But it was mostly because I did not know the real meaning of acceptance. *Hint:* It's probably not what you think it is either.

If I am to be truthful with myself, I was groomed early in life for acceptance. As a brown girl with full lips, a wide flat nose, and curly hair, at the young age of six I learned that the very features beloved and relished by my family would be the ones that some people would use in their attempt to devalue me. They were the reasons my first-grade teacher chose to try to stunt my potential. I didn't like it or agree with her, but I accepted that it wasn't my responsibility to change her mind. And she may never change it.

We spend days, months, yes, even years dwelling on things beyond our control—at least I have. Refusing to accept your whole story slows down your recovery from difficult situations and keeps you bobbing up and down, gasping for air, and drowning in suffering. A better option is to stop insisting that what is be any different than it is. Because all things cannot be changed—the sooner you accept it, the better your life will become.

What is acceptance?

The essence of acceptance is captured in a blog featured by *Awaken the Guru in You*: "What you resist persists, what you accept can heal."

Acceptance is not a vote of approval but rather an end to the protest. It acknowledges that your experience occurred without interpreting what happened, trying to fix it, or judging your feelings as being right or wrong. Acceptance pivots you away from guilt, malice, and bitterness to be able to reclaim power, peace of mind, and joy in your life. Although you cannot change the matter, you can grant yourself permission to co-exist with it. Because, as awful as it may have been, when you accept it, you can accept that you survived it.

Acceptance is the antidote for suffering

I've had my share of mental debates over things that were, for the most part, out of my hands—things that caused me more pain than accepting reality. As Shinzen Young says, "*Suffering* equals *pain* times *resistance*." And acceptance is by far the best antidote for suffering. What's more, it is inescapable if you desire to live well physically, mentally, and spiritually. But acceptance is a slippery bridge to cross—I continue to strive to make it my natural reaction.

The truth is, there are factors and fates outside your control—from everyday nuisances such as a delayed flight, traffic jams, sickness, and job termination to dreadful tragedies like the death of a loved one, betrayal, divorce, or being the victim of molestation or rape. You cannot always change what you go through, but you can decide *to be a casualty or to persevere.* When I've delivered an unfortunate diagnosis, some patients adamantly reject it—at the risk of their health—and others ask: "What can I do?" Neither resistance nor acceptance alters the diagnosis, but acceptance can change how you experience the outcome.

Acceptance is a life jacket

I understand that some days, a lot is coming at you and your emotions are constantly taxed by unpredictable circumstances. It can feel as though you're being dragged under by life's tumultuous currents. So how do you keep from drowning? I once read, "Throw your inner victim a life jacket." Acceptance is the life jacket that keeps you afloat.

1. Acceptance isn't for the faint of heart. Sometimes there are simply no do-overs. No matter how tight you close your eyes and wish otherwise, when you open them, your reality is still staring at you. So, what then? You can either cry over the spilled milk or clean it up. Here's an approach to accepting things you cannot change that'll help you avoid turning your world upside down.

2. *Acknowledge your feelings.* Stop sugar-coating or denying your true feelings—they're valid. Name and honor them. Be angry, disappointed, or sad. It takes courage to admit that you are *not* okay. Fabricating resilience by burying your pain is unhealthy. Allowing your feelings to run their course helps you understand them and heal from hurt. What feelings have surfaced from reading this chapter? Take a break to write them down.

3. *Address your feelings.* They won't disappear overnight, but if you stay committed to addressing what you feel, you'll

stop lugging emotional baggage around and move closer to acceptance. Use any healthy outlet of your choosing to work through them—a therapist, journaling, or practicing meditation. Start by finishing this sentence: A positive approach to this negative situation would be to . . .

4. *Focus on things you can change*. When you understand what you *can* control versus what you can't, then it is much easier to accept your current state and find your personal power. Your personal power comes from the things you *can* control. Center your attention where it can make a difference in your life—forgiveness, healing, and moving forward. Jot down a few things you do have control over.

5. *Have faith*. This is one of my super powers. Even if the initial intention of someone's behavior is to harm me, I use it for my own good—I look for the blessing in the mess. I've come to accept that sometimes the storm is the source of my strength. And though I wouldn't wish for what has happened to me or anyone else, I can decide not to be reduced by it.

You may not control
all the events that
happen to you, but you
can decide not to be
reduced by

them.

—Maya Angelou

PRESCRIPTION

For Acceptance

It may not be what you had hoped for, but it's the way the cookie crumbled. For the sake of happiness and harmony, learn to accept it so you can pick up the pieces and continue building your life. Let's work on acceptance one concern at a time. Repeat the following exercise as often as necessary.

• What is one thing in your life you need to accept?

• What is most difficult to accept about the situation and why?

- What can you control in this situation?

- What can't you control in this situation?

- What are concrete ways to focus on the things you can control? Name three.

- What can you do to deal with the things you cannot control? Name three.

5

FOR YOUR OWN
SAKE, FORGIVE

- What's showing up in life because you haven't forgiven past pain?

- Does offering forgiveness make you feel like you didn't matter?

Forgiveness is unlocking the door to set someone free, and realizing you were the prisoner.

—Max Lucado

Harboring ill feelings from the past damages you, not the person who harmed you. It eats at your soul. Resentment, anger, and jealousy bring your life to a standstill because you literally become stuck nursing painful emotions and picking at old wounds, preventing them from healing. Your grudges become badges worn as emblems of your suffering, and each one weighs you down and delays you from reaching your potential. Yes, forgiveness is a very generous gift to give to someone, especially if they hurt you deeply; however, they're not the beneficiaries of your forgiveness. You are.

Forgiveness is solely for you

Knowing this does not make it one bit easier to do. It's a hard hill to roll over. But you deserve better than to let the pain permanently define you. For me, initially, it fueled my anger to think of excusing someone for the harm they did to me. Eventually, the bitterness, coupled with my refusal to forgive, became a self-inflicted cruel and unjust punishment. And that, my friend, is far worse than deciding to forgive. After all, hanging on to the pain gives the person who wronged you more power. By not forgiving them, they're winning.

Forgiveness closes the book on whatever occurred. It stops you from reliving the pain. You get to rewrite the ending of the story. You become the survivor instead of the victim. And once you forgive your offender, you clear the way for self-forgiveness, which is the most rewarding gift you can give yourself.

It's not impossible

Hurts runs deep. Resentment can spread throughout your life like cancer, but there is no medicine better than forgiveness to cut it off at its roots. When I opened myself up to forgiveness, it gave me an overwhelming feeling of relief—as if I had been liberated. In that moment, I breathed new life.

Although forgiveness can feel like it is not doable, life will not require you to do the impossible. I remember praying for forgiveness for something I had done. I felt God gently nudge my heart to remind me that I was seeking something I was unwilling to give.

"And whenever you stand praying, forgive . . . so that your Father also who is in heaven may forgive you . . ." (Mark 11:25). Not a single day goes by without my needing forgiveness for a thought or for something I said or did. So how do I ask for what I won't grant?

Forgiveness doesn't require being asked

I was raised by a single mother. It wasn't of her choosing, but it was the circumstance created by my father's free will. He never explained why he chose to be absent in my life or why he never told me he loved me. For years I waited for a gesture from him that I could recognize as love. My father has since passed away, and I have had to forgive him without him offering me either remorse or regret. He died before I worked through my heartache, but I forgave my father to heal my life, not for him.

From my experience, forgiveness doesn't require being asked to do so. However, if you are waiting for a request, then listen inwardly, because your soul is always asking to be set free. Withholding forgiveness places your ability to heal in someone else's hands—that shifts the power away from you and keeps you in the role of a victim. Is that what your heart truly desires?

Why forgive?

Because when you do, life will feel much better. And you stand to reap huge benefits that will let you move forward. Some of them can be found tucked inside the word *forgive*:

F — *frees* your soul to heal

O — *opens* your heart to give and receive again

R — *reduces* depression, anxiety, and stress

G — *gives* your best life another chance

I — *isn't* condoning the wrongdoing, but living in peace in spite of it

V — *validates* your strengths

E — *ends* the fixation on revenge

Forgiveness is taking responsibility for how you allow your feelings about the past to shape your attitude toward life.

The truest signs of forgiveness

The truest sign of forgiveness is when you remember the person who wronged you, or recall the situation, but can leave behind the hostility and disappointment you once felt. And, taking it a step further, you wish them no ill-will. When I forgave my father, I placed the "pain" behind a veil in my mind where it was off limits to my heart.

Ask yourself: *Is holding on to the hurt worth selling your present and your future short?* For your sake, forgive.

"

Life becomes easier
when you learn to
accept the apology you

never got.

—Robert Brault

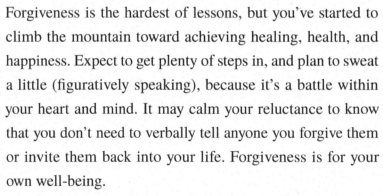

PRESCRIPTION

For the Ability to Forgive

Forgiveness is the hardest of lessons, but you've started to climb the mountain toward achieving healing, health, and happiness. Expect to get plenty of steps in, and plan to sweat a little (figuratively speaking), because it's a battle within your heart and mind. It may calm your reluctance to know that you don't need to verbally tell anyone you forgive them or invite them back into your life. Forgiveness is for your own well-being.

We are often hesitant to revisit personal pain; however, it is the place where healing and relief occurs. And your happiness depends on it. Take a deep breath and admit you're hurt. You don't have to keep pretending it didn't bother you. Acknowledging your pain isn't a sign of weakness. It just means forgiveness is in order. With that in mind, write your response to each of the following.

1. What's holding you hostage? Is it the disappointment of a parent, the rejection of a spouse, the betrayal of a friend, untold secrets, feeling forsaken? Be specific.
2. Why did it hurt you so much?
3. What do you need to forgive yourself for?
4. What did you learn about yourself from the disappointment you felt from being let down?
5. What is preventing you from making the decision to forgive?

In answering these questions, you will feel the heaviness that has weighed you down begin to slowly lift. Now, with that release, you can commit to forgiveness. Because it is the only way you can free yourself.

Time to celebrate!

Again, take a deep breath, hold it, and exhale. You're tackling some tough stuff. You are worth the work and effort—I'll believe it until you can believe it for yourself. Turn to the "Triumph" page and jot down hurdles you've overcome so far or ones you're ready to move past.

SCIENCE SAYS...

"Sixty-two percent of American
adults say they need
more forgiveness in their
personal lives."

—Survey, The Fetzer Institute

BE PRESENT

- What are you thinking about right now?

- Focusing only on the present, how could life feel and be better?

Learning to live in the present
moment is part of the path of joy.

—Sarah Ban Breathnach

Do you find yourself clicking the replay button and grieving over the past, or apprehensively anticipating the future? You aren't alone. Many people live life present in body only while their thoughts pace to and fro. However, letting bygones be bygones and welcoming the future in its due season is the best way to quit handing over your chance to be happy now.

I'm here, and this is now

You may already have the refrigerator magnet and the T-shirt reminding you to be present; yet, if you're like most of us, you probably still spend a lot of time wishing your days and life away. I confess that I've gone through the motions, caught up in thought, and not living life.

Kelle Yokeley's breathing exercise is a great tool to have at your fingertips when you find yourself looking back or looking ahead in life. There's no better time than the present to try it. Breath in and say to yourself, "I am breathing in." Breathe out, saying, "I am breathing out." On your next cycle of breath, say to yourself, "I am here. This is now." Repeat the entire mantra for a cycle or two (or three) until you're no longer lost in thought.

In this moment

If only for a brief moment, I encourage you to allow yourself to just *be*. Close your eyes, lower your shoulders, and sink into all this moment has to offer.

What sounds do you hear?

What aromas do you smell?

What are you envisioning in your thoughts?

What do you feel in your body?

Appreciate the stillness of right now.

An absolute blur

My entire medical school career is an absolute blur. When I wasn't focused on what was next, I was glancing back on how I could have done something better. From the start of medical school until I completed residency training, I held by breath until I was nearly depleted of oxygen and lifeless, waiting to live life once I became a doctor. What a grave sacrifice. I'm not sure—well, I am certain—there were parts of the journey I could have enjoyed. I was rarely present.

Be mindful

Mindfulness isn't just a popular self-help fix or sexy buzzword; it is a lifestyle tool that enriches your moment-to-moment experiences. It is about bringing your attention to the only *real* moment you have: this one.

The past is history (it cannot be rewritten), and the future is uncertain (it cannot be absolutely predicted). Do not clutter the here and now with what you cannot change and what you do not know for sure. The challenge is to find rays of joy in the present moment before it, too, becomes a part of the past.

There is a lesson, celebration, or unique experience in each moment.

I learn so much by spending time with my toddler niece. She isn't tethered to yesterday or overwhelmed with thoughts about tomorrow. Her focus is on what is right in front of her. Somewhere along the path to adulthood, we begin to frown upon this behavior. But this childlike view of life has *so* much merit.

A mindful life embodies the spirit of peace and lasting happiness. When you're conscious of the temporary nature of life—the ebb and flow—then the idea of living in the present is less intimidating because each moment brings new hope. There is richness and fullness packed into every single moment. There is a lesson, celebration, or unique experience in each one, even the unpleasant ones. I understand no one wants to seize a moment that's heavy with pain or resentment—I speak from experience. But in the present, be aware that even the darkest of nights end with the light of the sunrise. This realization makes it easier to live within the boundaries of the here and now.

How do you stop rewinding and skipping ahead in life?

Make the moments count.

1. *Reframe your thoughts into positive ones.* It's not entirely about what happened, but how you interpret what happened. This doesn't diminish the hardship you may have experienced; however, if you accept your

feelings about the abuse, heartbreak, or pain, then you can process and deal with them and not be held captive.

2. *Stop waiting for what's next.* Before we fully appreciate each milestone, we often turn our energy toward the next thing we want to accomplish. Embrace every moment as if it's the moment you have been waiting for—this is your moment to exhale, to celebrate, to live!

3. *Make mindfulness the admirable intention.* Living in the now is its own reward. Desire to be mindful because you accept that the current moment is the only place you can truly live—that's reason enough to stay present.

Don't let the sadness of
your past and the fear
of your future ruin the
happiness of your

present.

—Unknown

PRESCRIPTION 6

For Being Present

Are you ready for a laugh? Every time I read this quote, I chuckle:

> If you have one eye on yesterday, and one eye on tomorrow, you're going to be cockeyed today.
>
> **—Unknown**

Create your best life one moment at a time, starting with *this one*. Stop looking back at all the "wouldas," "couldas," and "shouldas." Don't waste today pondering over yesterday's mistakes—what a huge mistake that would be! Take a deep breath and center your thoughts on the present.

Let's practice the exercise from the beginning of this chapter. For the next 10 to 15 minutes, bring your attention to an object in your surroundings. If you lose focus, take a deep breath and gently center yourself again.

What does the space smell like?

What sounds do you hear?

What colors do you see?

What items standout?

What is the temperature?

What are your emotions?

What can you appreciate about this moment?

Make this activity a part of your everyday routine. It's a great way to override distractions that cause you to oscillate between backward and forward thinking, redirecting you to be present, now.

SCIENCE SAYS...

"Most of us spend nearly 47%
of our waking hours each day
thinking about something other
than what we're doing."

—Matthew A. Killingsworth and Daniel T. Gilbert.
"A Wandering Mind Is an Unhappy Mind,"
Science, 330: 932, 12 November 2010

7

H.O.P.E.
(HAVE ONLY POSITIVE EXPECTATIONS)

- Do you feel as though you've lost hope?

- What brings you comfort and hope?

> When the world says give up, hope
> whispers try it one more time.
>
> **—Anonymous**

We've all come to a place where it feels like life is stacked against us. Thank goodness that just because we feel a certain way doesn't necessarily make it so. Just because you feel hopeless doesn't mean you are without hope. Aren't you grateful that having hope is always an option? When my dear friend lost both parents and a brother within two years, lost her business, and nearly foreclosed on her home, she made the decision to not lose hope. And well, let's just say her life has turned a new leaf and she has her heart centered on positive exceptions in her life. Life is fragile, but a glimmer of hope can be your saving grace.

The heartbeat of your best life

The worst part of dark junctures on life's journey is feeling enclosed in hopelessness. Hope is what helps you brave life's twist and turns. It is tenacity—staying power, persistence, and determination. It's the mental and emotional fortitude to push through the pain of defeat and daily struggles. Hope is a powerful motivation that pulls you forward—even when you want to shut down—because deep down you know there is a bigger plan that will bring you out of your present state of despair. It is your internal torch that illuminates possibilities in your somber seasons. Hope is the heartbeat of your best life.

All hope is never lost

Despite our greatest efforts, from time to time we lose sight of hope. I've had my share of sleepless nights, my stomach in knots, tossing and turning in hopelessness and fear. I've had some experiences where "impossible" seemed like the only possible conclusion. I've prayed day and night for a divine miracle. Yet those bleak experiences were the best teachers. I learned that *all* hope is never lost—even when it means hanging on by a thread.

Hope is good for the mind, body, and spirit

A sense of hope is good for the *mind*. Psychologist C. R. Snyder wrote: "A rainbow is a prism that sends shards of multicolored light in various directions. It lifts our spirits and makes us think of what is possible. Hope is the same—a personal rainbow of the mind."

A sense of hope is good for the *body*. Hope is a restorative health tonic. I've observed and read reports that hopeful people experience better general health and vitality, including increased longevity, decreased rates of heart disease and depression, and improved tolerance for physical pain. Hope is at the center of wellness. It stimulates you to take the best care of yourself.

A sense of hope is good for the *spirit*. It's the sacred connection with the soul that gives you the confidence to thrive because your true strength is anchored in the Almighty (your Higher Power). When you feel hope, your heart is full and your spirit is renewed.

Keep hope alive

Where there is a will, there is a way to keep hope alive:

1. *Be your "Yes" in an ocean of "Nos."* People may say no, but you can refuse to be restricted and reduced by their limitations. Use skepticism and disapproval as a sign to be flexible and patient, nothing more and nothing less. Listen to your own heart and soul, because that's where your hope resides.

2. *Take the road less traveled.* Be a trailblazer! If the traditional blueprint doesn't work for you, draw up your own plans. At first, you may not be totally convinced of your road map, but keep following it until you trust it. As progress grows, so will your hope.

3. *Let go of being the victim.* Replace the word "victim" with "survivor." I know people who do this, and it fuels their ability to hope and look forward again. Be mindful, because there is a blurry line between hope and hoping for control over another's actions. As apparent as it may seem, sometimes the right thing doesn't make sense to other people. Don't waste your time trying to figure it out. Hope is personal.

4. *Talk with someone.* Avoid isolating yourself. You're not the only one who has been in your situation, and some people have already overcome your obstacles. Learn from their stories. ProjectHopeExchange.com is a great resource of people who have been in your shoes.

5. *Acknowledge the small victories along the way to your big dream.* Don't save the celebration until the end.

Actualized small hopes materialize big hopes. Taking bows along the way is encouragement to not give up, regardless of what is happening.

6. *Adopt a "this too shall pass" attitude.* Time really can heal and refresh hope. There are very few things that last a lifetime—things and people change and evolve. You're evolving right now by working through this book! Press ahead, there is sunshine in your forecast.

There's not one single thing life can throw at you that cannot be defeated with hope. Hold on.

We must accept finite
disappointment, but
never lose infinite

hope.

—Martin Luther King Jr.

PRESCRIPTION

For Strengthening H.O.P.E (Have Only Positive Expectations)

If your life is a far cry from what you hoped it would be, never ever give up. Because hope is necessary. It has a great deal to do with how you live your life and the parts of you that you dare release into the world. So let's keep hope bubbling within you.

1. Write down a challenge you have had in your life.

2. How did hope get you through the difficult time?

3. What are five ways that you cultivate and maintain hope?

4. Who are three people you draw hope from?

5. What roles does hope play in your everyday life, and what does it look like?

6. How do you inspire hope in others?

7. When you have hope, how do you behave differently?

PEACE AND HARMONY

- What do you envision when you think of inner peace?

- Where is lack of peace and harmony apparent in your life?

> Set peace of mind as your highest
> goal and organize your life around it.
>
> **—B. Tracy**

During one of our earnest and sincere conversations, my mother—in her more serious voice—shared that she would rather live in a one-room shack in peace than a mansion on top of a hill in conflict and confusion. What she taught me was that there's nothing in this world worth having without peace. No matter how grand it appears, it's an unfair trade. Peace is the most supreme reward and the highest joy. I am thankful for this pearl of wisdom from my mom. I didn't know then it would prove to be such a priceless gem.

Finding peace and harmony

Peace is always available even in the midst of chaos; choose it. It is not the conundrums and predicaments that arise in your life that steal your peace. Someone once said, "A ship is not necessarily destroyed by the water around it, but it is the water that gets into the ship that causes it to sink." It's what you let take root in your heart that is the real thief. Be mindful of letting your heart be a hiding place for conflict.

There was a time in my life when I would allow the smallest of issues to be a breach of peace, such as being ignored by the salesperson when, clearly, I was next in line or not receiving a thank-you for something I'd done. I would abandon harmony at a drop of a hat. But really, peace is too expensive a price to pay, even when you've been betrayed by a friend or made to feel invisible by a loved one. I've been there and done that. It took a toll on my mind, body, and spirit.

The unhealed me treated peace like a cheap thrill. The healed me has placed a high value on peace; other things are frivolous.

The more you seek and find peace and harmony, the harder it will be to lift the "Do Not Disturb" sign from your heart.

Peace and harmony keep you from being tossed around by life's light winds or blustery storms. It's an inside job that holds your life together no matter what is happening on the outside. It is true contentment.

Cultivate intentional peace and harmony
As a primary care doctor, I have taken care of terminally ill patients, and some—in spite of their health—have had a positive attitude. Outwardly, they looked nothing like what their bodies were going through. They managed to find peace in a dire state, and it showed. It was noticeable.

How can you intentionally cultivate peace and live in harmony? This is a BIG DEAL!

- Put a value on your peace. What you treasure, you'll fight to keep.
- Be unwilling to compromise your peace. It is non-negotiable.
- Live life one day at a time. It quiets anxieties about yesterday and worries of tomorrow.
- Let go of anything or anyone from your life that disrupts peace and harmony.
- Be quick to extend forgiveness (remember the earlier Prescription?). It lightens the heart and restores peace.
- Do not tie your peace to material things. It leaves you vulnerable.

- Accept what is not meant to be. Resistance blocks currents of peace.

- Do not build molehills into mountains. And don't let a mountain crush your spirits.

- Weed out what isn't bringing you tranquility and spend time on what does.

- Live and let live. Everyone is entitled to their own opinion.

- Develop a meaningful daily prayer life. You'll need help guarding your peace.

Constant awareness is what grants peace and harmony permission to have stillness in your life.

Create an inner P.E.A.C.E. plan

My personal P.E.A.C.E. plan—Pause, Examine, Act, Correct, and Exhale—shields me from unnecessary worries and being exhausted by life's problems.

- P = Pause: Put some distance between your feelings and conflict to reflect and reason through it.

- E = Examine: Look at the situation from all sides before jumping to a conclusion. Think it through.

- A = Act: What can you do to resolve the matter? If there is something you can do to bring a resolution to a problem, do it. If not, let it go.

- C = Change: What can you do differently to avoid similar instances? Being proactive preserves peace of mind.

- E = Exhale: Take a deep breath. Do not rehearse issues over and over in your mind. Move on.

You can adopt or adapt my plan or create your own peace treaty, one to quiet the heart and soul in a whirlwind of uneasiness and uncertainty. One where peace surpasses all understanding.

Peace can become a
lens through which
you see the world.
Be it.
Live it.
Radiate it out.
Peace is an

inside job.

—**Dr. Wayne W. Dyer**

PRESCRIPTION

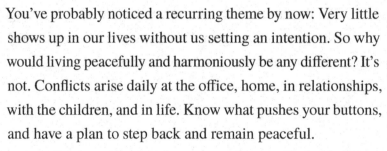

For Peace and Harmony

You've probably noticed a recurring theme by now: Very little shows up in our lives without us setting an intention. So why would living peacefully and harmoniously be any different? It's not. Conflicts arise daily at the office, home, in relationships, with the children, and in life. Know what pushes your buttons, and have a plan to step back and remain peaceful.

A walking meditation is a great way to calm and collect yourself and your thoughts. Here is a guide to get you on a path to peace and harmony.

- Set aside 10 to 20 minutes.
- Choose a quiet space to walk.
- Walk at a slow, natural pace.
- Let your hands and arms rest wherever is most comfortable.

- With each step, be conscious of lifting your foot from the earth and placing it back down.
- Keep a soft gaze on the ground a few feet ahead of you.
- When your mind wanders, guide it back to the act of walking.
- After three minutes of walking, shift your attention to your breath. Let it become the rhythm for your steps. Take three to four steps with each inhalation and exhalation.
- When you are ready, pause for one minute or so before turning around.
- In two-minute intervals, one at a time, expand your attention to sounds, smells, and what you see around you. Simply notice each sense.
- For the last two minutes, return your focus to walking. Notice your feet again. When you reach the end, stand still and take two slow, deep breaths.

9
UNMASKING EMOTIONAL FEAR

- What is your biggest fear?

- How are your fears holding you back from opportunities?

Courage is fear holding on a minute longer.

—Gen. George Patton

Your life is just as much a statement of your fears as it is your victories. Fears can cause you to settle for less than your purpose. Don't get me wrong; we all have fears, but we don't have to live in fear. And they don't have to run or ruin our lives.

The yin and yang of fear is that it's essential to live safely and, at the same time, bars you from living fully. On one hand it alerts and protects you from danger; on the other hand it can paralyze and incapacitate you. Fear comes in many different packages and can manipulate you in more ways than one: fear of being alone, fear of not being good enough, fear of embarrassment, fear of change, fear of the unknown, fear of heights, fear of financial disaster, fear of success, fear of abandonment. Everyone is afraid of something, but fear not—it's a sign that you're human.

The test is, will you empower or disempower your fears? The decision seems straightforward, but reality can cause the best of us to cave under the ever-present intimidation of the lies that fear tells you; don't believe them (not easy to do). Getting to the heart of the matter—the source, the root—stops fear from continuously interfering with your life and making you feel like your hands are tied, because they're not.

The seatbelt didn't fasten

One of my fears almost grounded me: the fear of the airplane seatbelt not fastening. And then, there I was on a return flight from Costa Rica, getting comfortable in my seat, when one of my greatest fears became reality: No matter how much I tugged at the seatbelt, I couldn't buckle it. The flight attendant offered me an extender and I wanted to crawl underneath the seat and die. I didn't. I refused the extender and flew home with the seatbelt pressed tightly into my stomach, etching a permanent tattoo on my soul as I took shallow breaths, because one deep breath would have caused more than the seatbelt to come undone. Fear can be a strong motivator to take action if you refuse to allow it to push you into inaction. (By the way, now the unused portion of my seat belt hangs down like a tail.) I decided to stop letting fear extend my pain.

Steps toward a fearless journey

All fears are not a figment of your imagination. As I alluded to earlier, some are undoubtedly justified and healthy. However real or blown out of proportion, fears can put a tight lid on your life because they won't let you get out of your own way to become who you dreamt you would be. Facing what genuinely frightens you head-on prevents it from running your life. How do you stand up to the very thing that causes you to shake in your boots, both figuratively and literally?

Step 1: Put your finger on it.

If you don't know there is a fire and where it is, you can't put it out, right? Fear surfaces and lingers when you can't exactly put your finger on what's eating at you. This is why it's important to identify your fears, where they are coming from, and bring them to light—no more secrets or feeling ashamed. Once you lean into your fears instead of away from them, they begin to loosen their hold and the ability to sabotage you recedes. This doesn't mean you won't experience nervousness or sweaty palms when your fears are triggered, but you won't run for cover, either.

Step 2: Take action to break free of fears

Knowing your fears is half the battle. Well, in this chapter, it's a fourth of the battle. But once you know your fears, you can break free and regain control so you aren't left standing motionless while adventures and opportunities pass you by.

There was a time when I let my fears disable me. Fear of being an entrepreneur, fear of not being married, fear of being judged, fear of not being respected in my profession, fear of not having children—they all pointed to my fear of failure. As it turns out, I was challenged to redefine failure, which freed me to go after my biggest goals. Having a deeper understanding of your fears makes them less scary. You likely won't overcome all of them, but you can prevent them from taking over your life.

Step 3: Cut off the power

Fear itself has no power; *you* are the power source. You ultimately determine if your fears will give rise to self-imposed limitations or you will build the confidence to hold a brave front against them. As long as you refuse to feed your fears, they stop draining your energy and stop threatening your dreams. Change the story you're telling yourself so that you are not the victim of your fears but, instead, your fears are a central part of your success.

Step 4: Embrace fear as the new normal

Surprised? I bet you didn't expect that as the fourth step! Embrace fear as the new normal. But don't let the emotion interfere with you living up to your fullest potential. Feel the fear, accept the discomfort, and do it anyway (even with your pulse thumping in your ear). When something is expected, you can possibly trade off a complete meltdown for some anxious jitters, which are much easier to work through. The long and short of it: Fear comes with the territory of shooting for the moon and landing on your own star!

Do the thing you fear
and the death of fear

is certain.

—Ralph Waldo Emerson

PRESCRIPTION

9

For Unmasking Emotional Fear

To stop fears from ruling your life, put a spin on them so they set you up to be your own smash hit. The four steps I've shared can help you balance fear with courage so that fear feels less overwhelming and more adaptable. Let's deliberately leverage fears so you can relaunch your life!

1. Put your finger on it.

   a. Expose your fears by writing down three of them. When they are out in the open, you will feel relieved. You don't have to start with your biggest ones; you can ease your way toward them.

   b. Why are you fearful of these things? When did the fear start?

   c. What is the *source* of your fears? (Blank) became a fear because of (blank).

2. Take action to break free of fear.

   a. Turn a negative into a positive. What are some of the positives that can come from confronting your fears?

   b. Be cautious of making a big deal over something that's not a big deal. What are the worst possible outcomes as they relate to the three fears you wrote down?

   c. If the worst-case scenarios happen, how can you handle each of them?

3. Cut off the power.

   a. How are you fears clouding your judgment and interfering with your goals?

   b. How can you use your strengths to work around your fears to accomplish your goals?

4. Embrace fear as the new normal.

   a. What are three things you can do to talk yourself off the ledge of fear? For example, in the heat of the moment, breathing exercises help me reduce fear.

   b. Moving toward fear instead of planning an escape route—there isn't one—is what guides you to the other side of fear. As you do a deeper dive into your three fears, ask yourself: Is your desire for the outcome greater than your fear?

Nice work, time to celebrate!

Wow, that was intense, but you did it! If you're still feeling some heaviness from the emotions you just invested, try releasing tension by doodling a little on one of the blank pages in the back of the book. Think of it as a palette cleanser for your emotional well-being.

 INTIMATE CONVERSATIONS WITH YOURSELF

- Do you say to others what you say to yourself?

- Why are you so harsh on yourself?

> 'I AM,' two of the most powerful
> words; for what you put after them
> shapes your reality.
>
> **—Bevan Lee**

~ 85 ~

Having conversations with yourself isn't necessarily the problem. Self-talk occurs every day, all day. It is what you *say* to yourself during those conversations that could be self-defeating. Be extra careful of the messages you send yourself. Handpick your internal words wisely and deliberately. They are the most influential words you will ever hear. You'll believe them—this holds true for both positive affirmations and negative self-criticism. In other words, the audio you rehearse within your mind will be crystallized in your external daily life. So, tell yourself something really good!

Your words carry weight

You learn how you really feel about yourself by paying very close attention to the way you talk and treat yourself. The intimate dialogues you have with yourself carry a lot of weight (they're more important than you'd imagine) and hugely contribute to shaping your self-image. What you affirm about yourself supersedes what others say about you. That's right—you really do have the last word!

Be kind within your mind

> *I can't believe that I'm not closer to being successful.*
> *No one appreciates me.*
> *I need to have it all figured out before I start.*

Reckless self-chatter shatters hope. Some of my worst defeats happened within my own mind. I didn't stand a chance against my negative thoughts and self-ridicule. It was an unfair fight. What a huge difference it made when my private discussions began to align with my aspirations. If being an author is a passion, I cannot tell myself that I will never write a book. After all, what I say to myself will either encourage or discourage me. What are your words bringing to life in your life?

You're your own personal coach

Think before you speak to yourself. Whether or not you signed up for the job, you're your own personal coach. Your life is a reflection of your voice. Victory—or defeat—starts with what you tell yourself, and your inner language can be your biggest opposition. Your personal pep-talk should be positive reinforcement of self-worth, self-respect, and self-esteem. If you can't speak kindly to yourself, remember: "Silence is a virtue."

The window crayons that changed my inner voice

On a late-night run to the store, I purchased a five-dollar box of window crayons that dramatically changed my morning conversation with myself. While standing in the front of the mirror, I've told myself some unkind and hurtful things: *You're not attractive. You're not successful. Your skin has too many blemishes.* Don't worry; I have since apologized to myself. Those window crayons came in handy with making amends. I had no idea then, but they switched my morning dialogue to much more kinder self-talk. I write it out so I can see it, say it, hear it, and believe it. And, oh boy, when I stopped telling myself the ugly things and got on my own side, I wouldn't let anyone else tell them to me either. I like me—no, I *love* me—and it's important that I let myself know by the way in which I speak to myself.

There's a video online that shows two friends sitting and talking. One of them says something horrible about herself, and the other says, "Imagine if you talked to anyone else the way you talk to yourself." Then the video shows her saying the unkind things to other people that she has said to herself. It didn't go well. At the end of the video, she says, "Yeah, I should be nicer to myself." Do *you* need to be nicer to yourself?

Your words matter

"Sticks and stones may break my bones, but words will never hurt me." This couldn't be further from the truth. Words do hurt, and they can sting even more when they're your own.

Your best life hinges on your every word. Affirmations are your personal library of self-compassion, kindness, love, and healing—your collection of positive mental notes. Since you'll have more conservations with yourself than anyone else, how can you become better at what you say?

1. Listen and filter negativity. Explore the root of your negative thinking. Do you notice any patterns?
2. Put a positive spin on it. For example, instead of saying, *I am fat*; rephrase it as, *I am going to eat healthier and work out to be more fit.*

3. Value your opinion above others. When I feel better about myself, the insensitive comments distract me less. Positive mantras help deflect any hurtful words of naysayers. My favorite one to repeat to myself is *I've been divinely created to be the fabulous and wondrous me.*

4. Treat yourself like a friend. It's easy to support loved ones even when they have made not-so-great choices. Give yourself the same benefit of the doubt.

5. Accentuate the positive. Negative news always travels faster than positive news. That doesn't have to ring true in your mind. Turn off harmful feedback with words of kindness.

Be careful how you're
talking to yourself,
because you are

listening.

—Lisa M. Hayes

PRESCRIPTION 10

For Intimate Conversations with Yourself

"I am [. . .]." It's enlightening when you understand that what follows those two little words makes a big difference in your life. It's a game changer! Follow these steps to start reprogramming your internal dialogue and to make loving and healthy self-talk a part of your daily internal conversation.

1. Each morning, greet yourself on a positive note, despite how you may feel. Say something kind to yourself. Start with "Good morning. You're awesome!" Or whatever uplifts you.

2. Next, take a moment to write down one or two of your positive traits. Save some for tomorrow, and the next day, and the day after that. Keep the positivity going daily!

3. Throughout the day, rehearse your affirmations and use them to encourage and motivate yourself. Each

member of my staff displays a word of the day at their workspace. It's encouraging to walk through the office and see them.

4. If you find yourself engaging in defeatist conversations—it happens to all of us—repeat your positive affirmations aloud. Write some down now so you're prepared to combat negative thoughts.

5. Practice this "thought-stopping" technique: Issue the command "Stop!" to verbally interrupt bothersome thoughts. It's like holding up a stop sign in your mind the moment you realize it's happening. For me, I simply say to myself, "STOP thinking that way; it's not true." If possible, say it aloud. The more you use it, the less you'll need it over time.

11

ALL THINGS GRATEFUL

- When is the last time you counted your blessings?
- What gives your life energy?

Gratitude starts a chain reaction
to happiness.

—**Unknown**

Whenever I would receive a gift or token of kindness, my mother would immediately look at me and ask, "What do you say?" And she waited for me to reply, "thank you." There is a difference between being polite and being grateful, but expressing thanks is definitely a start.

Gratitude is when "thank you" doesn't feel like enough. It's not simply a nice gesture. The more I experience it, the more persuaded I am that it really doesn't have anything to do with the size of the gift but with how I value the thought behind the gesture.

The thank-you note

I honestly didn't realize how powerful the influence of gratitude was until my simple thank-you note sparked one of my most meaningful friendships, with my now mentor, Dr. Howard Murad. We hadn't met when I sent him a letter to express my sincere appreciation for his creation of a skincare line that transformed the appearance of my skin. It was so well received that I was gifted products and later an invite to attend one of his wellness retreats. I had a fabulous time, which could only be outshone by an invitation to visit the Murad corporate office and attend L.A. Live! Since then, he has been dear to me, and I'm included in his scrolling pictures of his family and friends—it warms my heart. An ever-grateful attitude captures the pure essence of every moment of life. You may even end up with a new friend!

What is gratitude?

Author William Stone once said, "Big doors swing on little hinges." Gratitude is one of those little hinges that opens big hearts. Your awareness turns from what's missing and imperfect to blessings and goodness.

Gratefulness is life-affirming and will quiet negative thoughts. When you live a life of gratitude, joy and happiness are not fleeting, and you have fewer regrets. A heart full of gratitude invites you to experience life's miracles every single day. It's not that you're wearing rose-colored glasses; you are simply choosing to focus on the roses rather than the thorns.

When life is challenging, gratitude is the ray of light peeking through the thick clouds. Being thankful helps you balance the ups and downs. Make it a habit and you'll have far more happy days, because when you're grateful, life gives back more.

You can start being grateful now

What if gratitude became a never-ending, uninterrupted feeling that isn't just in response to big things? Instead of being annoyed about the old car, frustrated about your job, or fed up with the cramped apartment, look for what you *do* have, and be grateful for it: a car, a job, and an apartment. There is nothing wrong with desiring more from life, but do not discount the good things that are right in front of you.

Make room to open your mind and heart. Finish this sentence: I am thankful for_____. Doesn't it feel nice to remind yourself of what you have now? You don't have to chase it or wait for it, just recognize that it's here!

Be grateful for it all

When the storms of life come crashing down, they test your gratitude. During difficult times, although it can seem out of reach, you have the most to gain from being grateful. Gratitude is unconditional. When you are disciplined about living gratefully, the spirit of being appreciative isn't contingent on whether you are in a blissful or a melancholy season of your life.

We all have felt drained by life. Gratitude breeds healing. Gratitude breeds strength of mind. Gratitude breeds hope, clarity, resiliency. Be grateful; it all works for your benefit—the mountain highs and the valley lows.

It is a choice to be grateful

Gratitude has little to do with what you have or don't have, but everything to do with how you *choose* to live your life. Whether you are distracted by things that elude you or you decide to take nothing for granted—including the very air you breathe—is up to you, but living with gratitude as your filter makes a big difference. What I appreciate most about being grateful is that it not only magnifies the good in others but also amplifies the good in each of us.

When seeds of thankfulness are nurtured, you connect with the world on a higher plane, one where the wholesomeness and humaneness of being thankful are the focus. Even so, living above your circumstances and emotions isn't always easy. But it is a choice—*your* choice—to be grateful.

Gratitude is nature's pick-me-up. It won't fix everything, but it will make a whole lot of things feel much better. To live happier, make gratitude your default setting—where you intuitively engage with life and focus on what you have, instead of what you think you deserve. To be grateful is to be mindful, and mindfulness is the backbone of happiness. Simply said: Gratitude is your access to all the goodness that is in your life.

"

Gratitude is a vaccine,
an antitoxin,
and an

antiseptic.

—John Henry Jowett

"

PRESCRIPTION

For Choosing Gratitude

11

To strengthen your capacity for gratitude, count your blessings. Pay attention to the details that make your life great, and intentionally choose to be grateful for them. David Steindl-Rast's "Stop. Look. Go." technique is a powerful way to live with heartfelt gratitude.

- *Stop* means slow down and get quiet.
- *Look* mean to use your senses: See, smell, listen, touch, taste.
- *Go* means to take action to intentionally respond—chose your answer—to the moment.

Now try and use that method.

1. You should "Stop. Look. Go." each day. Form the habit by deciding what will trigger you to pause. It could be when you first awaken, when you have a cup of coffee,

closing a door at the end of a workday, each time you enter a specific room. Then, look and go. To get started, write down your trigger.

2. Notice how this technique kindles gratitude. Note the small things you are now more aware of as a result of "Stop. Look. Go." Keep a journal of your experience.

3. Express gratitude toward others daily. In a note, text, email, or phone call, share with someone (at least one person) why they are important to you.

4. Gratitude is given and received. Look for moments to share a small act of kindness *weekly*. Keep a journal of your actions so you can be reminded of goodness.

12

JUST
BREATHE

- Have you ever taken a moment to observe your breathing?

- Do you breathe fully into your belly and engage your diaphragm?

Smile, breathe, and go slowly.
—Thich Nhat Hath

There really isn't anything more natural than breathing, yet most of us aren't very good at it. Learning the art of breathing—cleansing of the mind, body, and spirit—can literally change your life. It has for me!

You might be asking, *What's the big deal?* I did too when I was introduced to breathwork, but it *is* a huge deal. Your breath is more powerful than you realize, especially conscious, deep belly breathing (which is when the diaphragm is activated). Breathing with intention relaxes the body, focuses the mind, and allows you to sink deeper within to intimately connect with your spirit.

Experience real breathing

Think of each breath as a brief recess from whatever is happening and a chance to choose your reaction: to regain self-control or to bask in the moment. A pause on purpose to take a deep breath is also a way to be mindful of bringing closure to one encounter before starting another—so that, in particular, unpleasant experiences aren't projected onto someone innocent.

A shortcut (or should I say, an easily accessible approach) to calmness and being centered is conscious breathing—it engages your lungs, ribcage, and belly. Now, stop in this moment, inhale deeply, hold the breath, and slowly exhale through your mouth; try it a couple more times. Feel that release as you let the air in and out? If you don't, keep practicing and you'll get it.

The untapped power of breathing

At the peak of stress, my breaths were shallow, rapid, and irregular. Before I mastered how to harness the power of my breath, life's hurdles and liabilities could potentially precipitate a tailspin. But when I discovered the dynamic capacity of deep breathing, I was able to slow down, compose myself, and decide how I would allow life to affect me. As songwriters Rob Greaney and Mel Rattray elegantly said, "Not every raindrop is a storm." Conscious breathing adds space between a distressful situation and my (or your) reaction, skirting a downpour (or at least providing an umbrella).

What is your breath communicating to you?

Without trying to change it, pay attention to its rhythm and sound as you inhale and exhale. The quality of your breathing provides hints about how you're really feeling in the moment, so don't overlook them. Is your breathing quiet and flowing with ease? Or do you feel resistance? My favorite thing is to couple conscious breathing with a body scan (a mental scan up and down the body) to bring awareness to any tension that my body needs to let go. It's a medication-free way to recover from headaches and body aches, or perhaps the breath is the medicine.

You always have it with you

One of the many benefits of using your breath to create wellness is that it's always at your disposal—available anytime and anywhere. It's good that you don't have to put a lot of thought into breathing. But if you purposely think every now and then to *fully* breathe, you could not only change the tempo of your breath but also the tempo of your life. You could take a break from the fast track and slow life down long enough to truly catch your breath.

A breath of wellness

Obviously, it's impossible to live without breathing, but it is possible, sadly, to live without experiencing the restorative and healing power of your breath. Sometimes one or two breaths are all you need, but some stress requires six or seven deep breaths. I am continually pleasantly surprised by how the act of completely emptying my lungs unloads stress, restores balance, and redirects my thoughts. It never fails that I am rewarded with renewed energy after each deep inhalation and slow exhalation.

Mindful breathing makes life feel a bit lighter. Each time you pause for a cycle of deep belly breathing, you are overriding anxiety about what has happened and are, instead, choosing to focus on what *is* happening. Over time, you'll become a natural at letting your breath do the work and being calmer in your reactions. But for now, take another deep breath. Ready? Breathe—inhale deeply, hold it, and exhale slowly. Whatever life is handing you, breathe through it.

If I had to limit my
advice on healthier
living to just one tip,
it would be simply to
learn how to breathe

correctly.

—Dr. Andrew Weil

PRESCRIPTION

For Just Breathing

Why all the hype about breathing? I like how this title from an article phrased it: "Your breath is your brain's remote control." Deep belly breathing lets you stop clicking through the different channels of your life, hit the pause, and purge emotional debris.

For me, the art of mindful breathing has supported physical recovery, spiritual peace, and emotional healing, helping me to feel more fulfilled.

There are several styles of breathwork. Select one that works best for you, then set your intention to practice daily. My preference is the 4-7-8 breathing exercise by Dr. Andrew Weil. Give it a try. If you find the counting more hindering than helpful, leave it off.

1. Close your eyes.
2. Prepare to take a deep breath; and expand you belly, ribcage, and lungs.
3. Breathe in through your nose for four (1-2-3-4) counts.
4. Hold the breath for seven (1-2-3-4-5-6-7) counts.
5. Audibly blow out the breath for eight (1-2-3-4-5-6-7-8) counts.
6. Repeat for four cycles.

You can confidently face life's biggest challenges if you don't allow them to take your breath away. Ready? *Breathe.*

SCIENCE SAYS...

"Different emotions are linked to different patterns of breathing, and so changing your breath can change how you feel."

—P. Philippot, G. Chapelle, and Sylvie Blairy.
"Respiratory feedback in the generation of emotion,"
Cognition and Emotion, 2002, 16(5): 605–627.
Published online 9 September 2010.

13

BELIEVE IN YOURSELF

- What do you believe about yourself?

- Is what you believe about yourself true?

She believed she could, so she did.

—**R. S. Grey**

In the *Wonderful Wizard of Oz*, Dorothy believed she could close her eyes and click her heels three times to return home. You're likely not trying to get to Kansas, but wherever life is taking you, it is powered by what you believe. You may have doubts, that's normal. And it may not always pan out exactly as you thought it would; that's life. And yes, catastrophes will happen; get up, dust yourself off, and still believe. Believing in yourself does not mean being free of all doubts and misfortunes; it means moving forward with all-out efforts in spite of them, knowing you've got everything it takes!

Believing is one of my superpowers

Even as a child, I knew believing was one of my superpowers (yes, I have more than one—and you probably do too) to live the life I wanted. Believing that you have a superpower can actually help you turn a natural ability into something powerful. It's been said, "No one is you, and that is your superpower." I agree!

Financially, when I was growing up, my family was classified as lower socioeconomic. Even so, my beliefs about what was possible for my life were exponentially greater than my family's means—mainly because my mother stressed not to put up roadblocks where there weren't any and believe in myself. I took that lesson to heart. As an African-American female physician, sure intelligence, resources, and opportunities were an asset, but there is nothing more valuable than believing in yourself—it's your true measure of wealth. When dream crushers try to shatter your vision, your inner self must have the boldness to tenaciously cry out—either aloud or silent-ly—"That's not what I believe!"

You're the master of your own fate, and your highest purpose in life is paved by self-confidence. All things are possible for those who have faith in their own judgment and abilities.

Unlearn false truths

What is one thing you have always believed to be true about yourself? What if it isn't? Some things you believe about yourself simply are not true, so you must unlearn false truths. Really think about that for a moment.

What are false truths? They are the stories of not measuring up. The messaging, cultural conditioning, and programming by those closest to you, media, and institutions you may have embraced as your own beliefs. False truths are the tales ingrained in your subconsciousness that have deceived you. The self-lies telling you that you can't when you know darn well you can. It's time to purge the fabrications!

This moment is a chance to start with a blank slate to rework your thoughts. We form a belief by accepting a statement or opinion as fact. Therefore, to unlearn something is to stop believing assumptions about you, and outdated versions of you, not based on facts. For example: "You don't have what it takes!" Says who? People can say whatever they want, but it doesn't mean that it's true. It only becomes true when you believe it. The way to banish false truths is to discard what isn't factual. Letting go can seem like you're losing your sense of self, but remember, that's not the *real* you. Untruths about yourself are the best things you will ever *un*learn.

Get to know your truths

There is no one more important for you to trust than yourself. When you believe in your purpose and abilities, and accept that you will make mistakes and have rejections, the hardest part is done. So stop second-guessing yourself. If only it were that easy, right? It's not. But here's a way to start sincerely believing in yourself.

1. *Get to know your true self.* It's easier to believe in people who you know. Become so familiar with your inner voice, you can distinctly hear it over doubts. Ask yourself:
   - Who are you right now? It may be totally different from who you used to be.
   - What do you want out of life? Perhaps, it has changed.
   - What do you admire in yourself? I'm sure there is a lot that sparkles inside of you.

   Keep asking questions until you know yourself better than you ever did before.

2. *Be honest with yourself.* Being truthful about what you feel, value, and desire builds trust. It also positions you to advocate for yourself.

3. *Trust your own decisions.* You'll make some wrong ones, but you'll also make a lot of right ones. We desire approval for the simplest—what we wear, for

example—to the most momentous decisions—how we should live our lives. While it's okay to talk through things with others, make sure the final decision is yours.

4. *Acknowledge your strengths and your weaknesses.* Believing in yourself means not hiding any part of yourself. You must be comfortable in your own skin—blemishes and all.

5. *Think twice about following the crowd.* Question what you have been told by asking, *Is it true?* People can be very persuasive, but you'll feel less conflicted when you know your own truth.

Once we believe in
ourselves, we can
risk curiosity, wonder,
spontaneous delight,
or any experience that
reveals the human

spirit.

—E. E. Cummings

PRESCRIPTION

For Believing in Yourself

13

Have you heard of a team-building activity in which a person is asked to fall backward, totally trusting in the team to break their fall? What enormous confidence in others! This is the same extraordinary belief you must have in yourself.

Let's work on self-confidence building by looking at who makes the decision in your life. A word of caution: Do not be quick to circle "me." Do so only if you make a particular decision by yourself or with the help of a trained professional. If you make it with friends or media influencers, the appropriate response is "me & others." Lastly, if it's a decision where you take little credit, the best answer is "mostly others." There's no judgment, just insight to help you believe in yourself.

Who makes the decision?

My favorite book?	Me	Me & Others	Mostly Others
What I eat?	Me	Me & Others	Mostly Others
Which restaurants I dine at?	Me	Me & Others	Mostly Others
Where I work out?	Me	Me & Others	Mostly Others
Which friends I have?	Me	Me & Others	Mostly Others
What my social activities are?	Me	Me & Others	Mostly Others
Where I shop?	Me	Me & Others	Mostly Others
What I wear?	Me	Me & Others	Mostly Others
What my ideal weight is?	Me	Me & Others	Mostly Others
What career I pursue?	Me	Me & Others	Mostly Others
Which organizations I'm a member of?	Me	Me & Others	Mostly Others
Who I should be in a relationship with?	Me	Me & Others	Mostly Others
Where I should live?	Me	Me & Others	Mostly Others
What car I drive?	Me	Me & Others	Mostly Others

—Adapted from *Confidence Activities*
(polk-fl.net/community/volunteers/documents/
ymConfidenceActivities.pdf)**, Polk Mentoring Alliance,
2008; revised 8/2008**

Well done, time to celebrate!

This Prescription may have brought you face-to-face with self-doubt, but hopefully you can now start rebuilding your self-esteem. Remember to trust yourself. That, in itself, is its own reward!

14

MEDITATE DAY AND NIGHT

- How can you integrate meditation into your daily routine?

- During meditation, how do you focus your mind?

> Quiet the mind, and the soul will speak.
>
> **—Ma Jaya Sati Bhagavati**

I chuckle when I think about my initial experience with meditation. I had low expectations. I didn't believe the idea of being still would bring about some sort of mind-body-spirit connection. Not to mention, *Who has the time?* I thought, *I barely have time to be still for 30 seconds, much less 30 minutes or an hour.* With such reluctance, I am not certain why I decided to try meditation, but I did. At first I spent more time thinking about my to-do list than actually meditating. My thoughts wandered all over the place. Ha!

My how things change. After much practice, I greet this much-needed space with open arms. I am very grateful for a daily break to slow my thoughts and be intentional about taking care of *me*. Each time I sit still with myself, I'm guided to a place of self-discovery where I get to know and understand myself just a tad better. Through meditation, I've come to realize, as with most things, it's not the quantity of time but the quality of time. I am (you are) free to return to the busyness of life whenever I (you) chose; however, before I know it, even an hour of meditation feels like mere minutes. What a one-eighty!

You'll thank yourself
With all the responsibilities and obligations on your checklist, an interlude of stillness probably sounds frivolous. Let me assure you, it's not. Whether it's five minutes or an hour, the quiet subtle beauty of meditation elevates your approach to life. It trains the mind to be more present and stimulates concentration, thereby inspiring better choices and, in turn,

increasing creativity and productivity. What's more, meditation switches the mood from frustrating to calm, and the physical health benefits are plentiful too. It's a life-altering practice!

But like many simple things, we often make them more complicated than they are while also discounting their value. Our focus tends to be on what is required from us (a momentary breathing space) instead of the blessings we'll receive. There is a wealth of personal rewards in cultivating genuine peace and healing through meditation.

Food for the soul

Meditation is good food for the soul. It tapers the overload of thoughts, soothes the soul, settles the mind, and helps you to relocate your center. The quality of your life rests on the quality of your thoughts. Stillness clears headroom so you can travel beneath the surface of your thinking to the root of your feelings and better regulate your emotions, which positively impacts how you interact with the world and yourself. Meditation is a building block for more happiness. That's both gratifying and fulfilling!

The art of being and living

Meditation is not a religion, and it's also so much more than closing your eyes and breathing. It infuses your life with good energy. Meditation is the art of being and living.

Although an extreme measure, studies show that people who take a vow of silence experience remarkable feelings of positivity and high levels of thought. It is also said that they, through meditation, feel less physical pain in general due to their heightened sense of being. Quiet time with yourself is more than a "feel good" exercise. Intentional stillness reduces the negative influences of stress, decreases anxiety, increases happiness, and improves health.

When I am tossing and turning in bed, it's usually because my mind is in overdrive or I'm in an emotional wrestling match about something. Turns out that on those restless nights, meditation slows racing thoughts, allows them to pass without judgment, and lets me be less bothered by small things (and even curtails the bigger ones), all of which lulls me into a peaceful night's sleep.

An inner vacation

The notion of meditation being an "inner vacation" is a wonderful description to sum up the rewards of this restorative practice. You don't have to travel to a far-off exotic place to take time away from preoccupying thoughts and the busyness of life. You can take a trip anytime you wish; simply be still, retreat from the world around you, and meditate.

When you meditate,
you give yourself
an inner

vacation.

—Swarmi Rama

PRESCRIPTION

For Meditating Day and Night

Our hectic lives can leave us disconnected from ourselves. Meditation restores the connection. A bonus: There's more than one correct way to meditate. A good way to begin is with guided meditation, which is when a trained practitioner supports you (virtually or in person). A quick search on YouTube or apps such as Headspace and Calm can be a great introduction. Start with five minutes. You'll notice when you are ready to increase your time commitment. If sitting still doesn't appeal to you, try a quiet walk, slow stretches, or coloring—any activity that calms your mind and centers your thoughts is a form of meditation.

Find a place where there will be no interruptions. Set the mood with your favorite candle, a mat or cushion, a timer, and music. Keep the room's decor modest. Too many items can cause distractions. Once your space is ready, try this option for a short meditation:

1. Turn on some soft music and light a candle.

2. Start the timer.

3. Take a seat or lie down on the floor.

4. Close your eyes.

5. Breathe deeply and slowly through your nose and exhale through your mouth. Place your hand over your stomach to notice each breath, and imagine it flowing throughout your body.

6. Let your mind travel to a place of calmness.

7. Select a positive affirmation and rehearse it in your mind. When your thoughts wander (I've caught myself making a grocery list a time or two), just softly repeat your affirmation.

8. Before opening your eyes, gently bring your focus back to the room.

9. Remain seated for a few minutes; notice how you feel, and think about how to keep the experience present throughout your day.

SCIENCE SAYS...

"Meditation can reduce the wake time of people with insomnia by 50%."

—Ong J, Sholtes D.
"A mindfulness-based approach
to the treatment of insomnia."
Journal of Clinical Psychology,
November 2010, 66(11): 1175–84

15

SPIRITUAL WELLNESS

- When was your last spiritual check-up?

- Do you have a spiritual wellness plan?

"Spirituality is the science of the soul.
—**Swarmi Vivekananda**"

A person cannot live by bread alone, because we are not only physical bodies but also spiritual beings. Most certainly, even before reading this book, you were familiar with the collective use of the terms "mind," "body," and "spirit." That's because they work in tandem to create total well-being. As mental health affects the physical, and the physical affects the mental, spiritual wellness is intricately linked to them both.

A bridge between the mind and heart

Spiritual wellness is availing yourself to intimately connect with a higher power. This awakens a level of consciousness that serves as a moral compass to live authentically, aligned with your purpose, and at peace within yourself. It harmonizes your humanity—who you are in the universe—with your guiding beliefs and who you are individually, thereby cultivating wholeness.

Spiritual wellness builds a bridge of contentment between the mind and the heart. It is not synonymous with religion. But, it does encompass your relationship with God or your source of absolute being. In matters of the spirit, there is a breadth of practices such as meditation, prayer, yoga, communing with nature, art therapy, volunteerism, and the like which provide diverse paths to ensure all is well with the soul. Spiritual wellness is that inner quiet space where you are a perpetual student of your character and your calling—your life's purpose.

Virtues of spiritual wellness

Your faith, values, beliefs, principles, and ethics make up your spiritual DNA. They are the distinctive qualities you contribute to make the world a better place and what inspire you to be your best self. Your spirit is the heart of your essence. Expressing compassion, offering and receiving love, granting forgiveness to yourself and others, seeking personal fulfillment and greater good, confidently knowing your beliefs, and trusting your divine intuition are the virtues of spiritual wellness that move the needle of joy and oneness in your life. Living in such a way that you are true to yourself enhances your ability to cope with physical and mental pressures. And it shines a more optimistic light on life.

Knowing there is something bigger

A healthy spiritual life steers you toward an enlightening quest of self-inquiry and self-discovery. To emphasize an earlier point, it is the part of your life's journey where you make a truce with everything and everyone *outside* of yourself to live in harmony *within* yourself.

A sound relationship with your spirit unveils who you are and why you are here. In other words, the meaning of your life is revealed. Don't we all yearn for such an epiphany? For me, the most uplifting aspect of being spiritually grounded is knowing that there is something much bigger than myself. Something greater than the concrete world I inhabit. Something that sustains and supports me. Something that balances my soul's needs with my physical ones. Being mindful of these rewards helps me to walk the fine line of being selfless yet fulfilled.

Conditioning your spirit

Spirituality is palpable. It's tangible, not mystical. It is generally the most neglected and estranged dimension of ourselves. This is partly because we do not routinely nurture our spirit. However, negligence doesn't forfeit the relevance and dynamic clout spiritual wellness has on our real lives.

Being spiritually out of shape means you run the risk of physical and mental imbalance, especially because they intimately tie in together. When I lost more than 140 pounds, I altered my eating and workout habits, but the secret to my success was being in my best spiritual condition. It was exercising my willpower muscle—by sticking to a regimen of meditation, prayer, solitude, journaling my thoughts and emotions, releasing residue of hurt feelings, and healing my relationship with food. Apart from this, I learned to recognize physical cravings versus soul cravings. These fixes, alongside lifestyle changes, lifted the weight. Embracing spiritual alternatives to overeating trained me to become spiritually fit by developing the wisdom and confidence to address life differently. I could see, feel, and hear the world more graciously and empathetically. Conditioning my spirit renewed my thinking and endurance to do the work to lose the weight as well as drop the baggage I wasn't meant to carry.

The spiritual element of wellness is in the eye of the beholder. How it translates in our lives is unique to each of us. But its far-reaching influence flows over into every aspect of our being. Spiritual wellness is an olive branch of peace between our inner and outer lives that creates an oasis for us to thrive to fulfill our purpose!

"

Spiritual wellness
is about creating
a greater sense of
personal greatness,
inner-joy, connection
to spirit and the world
around you each and

every day.

—**Dr. Dolores Fazzino**

PRESCRIPTION 15

For Spiritual Wellness

Are you spiritually deconditioned? When is the last time you gave any serious thought to your spiritual health? One of the healthiest things you can do for yourself is to be as vigilant about your spirituality as you are about your mental and physical well-being.

How often do you skip meals? It's rare to pass on a snack much less a meal, yet days, weeks, months, and even years can go by without a morsel of spiritual nourishment. So let's work out your daily conditioning plan to get you divinely fit!

1. To warm up, make a list of activities or practices that rouse your spirit. For example, gardening, volunteering, positive affirmations, cleaning (go figure), or attending church.

2. Every day, before heading out into the world, *stretch* your mind, body, and spirit to get in touch with your purpose and make the day meaningful. How can you include one of your spiritual practices as a part of your morning routine? Perhaps take a moment to write something affirming on your bathroom mirror (I keep a box of window crayons on my vanity), sit quietly to mediate, or pause to say a prayer.

3. Preserve your strength. Create a few 5- to 10-minute midday rituals to check in with your inner self. This is a great time to do a breathing exercise from an earlier Prescription: Inhale, hold the breath, exhale. Choose activities that don't require a big to-do so they can easily fit into your day.

4. Generosity, goodness, and charity are spiritual treadmills that open the door to share who you are with others. They're the best cardio workouts to elevate your soul. What activities or volunteerism can you do at least twice a month to really get your heart pumping?

5. Building endurance is essential to being spiritually fit. We are always growing and discovering ourselves on a deeper level. What can you put in place for motivation and discipline to stay in good spiritual shape? I do gratitude journaling to help me with this.

16

A STRONG SPIRITUAL CONNECTION

- Are you conscious of your spiritual well-being?

- How do you keep the connection with your spirit alive?

> Spirituality lies not in the
> power to heal others, to perform
> miracles, or to astound the world
> with our wisdom, but in the ability
> to endure with the right attitude
> whatever crosses we have to face in our
> daily lives and thus rise above them.
>
> —Sri Daya Mata

Is this it? Is this all there is to life? From time to time, this conversation has taken up residence in my inner space. I grappled with whether I'd reached the top of my pinnacle in regard to fulfilling my purpose. More often than not, the unrest stemmed from a strong desire for a deeper meaning of life. My soul's light needed to be turned back on, because it was flickering out.

It's all too easy for the outside world—where the focus is on people, places, and things—to block access to your soul's consciousness. You lose the interconnectedness of the mind, body, and spirit when you steadily try to satisfy your spirit without seeking its guidance. Your soul is the truth of who you are. It cannot be deceived. It so desperately wants to be interwoven in every aspect of your life in order to reveal the best version of yourself; however, you must intentionally welcome its spiritual Prescriptions—the instructions to your higher self. Life is good when you have oneness with your soul.

A broken connection

"Can you hear me now?" We are born connected to our spirits, but through trauma and social conditioning, we begin to lose contact. As a result, our spirits and bodies become out of sync, which is why we find ourselves filled with confusion, doubt, regret, shame, impatience, sadness, and anger. This emotional imbalance causes us to live in a way that doesn't serve us mentally, physically, or spiritually. The broken connectivity is also the reason we disguise our authentic self from society (and sometimes from ourselves), struggle with trusting our intuition, and either handover our power or obsessively feel the need to control everything.

The origin of the disconnection

We've all been there before; seasons of feeling spiritually lackluster is a natural part of life. Don't beat yourself up; I've felt that way too. And we're not alone. In those moments, ask yourself: Who or what interrupted your interconnection? Knowing where the wiring is faulty helps you recover from spiritual lethargy and reactivates your inner power. Was it:

- Opening your heart to negativity?
- Becoming side-tracked on a path that wasn't yours to travel?
- Holding on to pieces and parts of you that don't fit you anymore, or never did?
- Spending little time practicing spirit disciplines?
- Suppressing instead of healing pain, which left you in a place of suffering?
- Not trusting your divine instincts?
- Judging your purpose against everyone else's?

Singling out the origin of your spiritual disconnection restores the circuit between mind-body-spirit so that you can plug back into the true essence of your life. Ask yourself: *What is your spiritual barrier?*

Spiritual imbalance pushes back on moderation

Living removed from yourself and your life has serious repercussions. The longer you stay in a spiritual drought, the more inclined you are to push back on moderation. Consequently, unhealthy addictions creep in, such as drugs, alcohol, food, sex, shopping, social media, and even exercise. They're reckless attempts to fill the gap of spiritual isolation and to try to feel connected to something, even when that something isn't good for you.

Your mental state can also give you signs that there's a defective spiritual connection. Psychological illnesses such as anxiety, depression, and eating disorders could be signals that you have a short in your spiritual circuit.

Nothing is a substitute for being in harmony with your whole self and your higher power. It's spiritually awakening!

Becoming spiritually alive

Beneath our bodies, beneath our minds, flows the pureness of our spirits. It is never apart from us, but because we live in a culture where there is ongoing competition over superficial things, we aren't always engaged and listening.

Becoming spiritually alive forges an alignment with a much deeper meaning of life; you honor the desires of your heart. You know yourself better. You know you're doing what you are supposed to be doing. You know it is going to work out for your favor—no matter the outcome. You know that there is something beyond yourself merging your body and spirit on your life path. You know it because you feel it in your soul; you feel it in your bones!

When we are
spiritually fit and
balanced we are a
powerfully exquisite
blend of human
fallibility and divine
perfection. It is this
dynamic tension
that gives us our
uniqueness, our power
to create and our

compassion.

—Caroline Reynolds

PRESCRIPTION 16

For a Strong Spiritual Connection

A strong spiritual connection is to the soul as food is to the physical body, and as peace is to the mind. When spirituality takes center stage in your life, who you are meant to be becomes front and center. This being so, let's get in touch with your spiritual side.

1. What three activities make you feel spiritually grounded? Where could you easily fit them into your day? Prayer, meditation, and devotional readings are on the top of my list. Whatever helps you tap into your soul, use it to frame your day. In other words, each day find 5 to 10 minutes here and there to pull out your spiritual toolbox and tighten the pipeline to your soul. Perhaps it's as simple as greeting the daybreak with gratitude or going on a morning stroll.

2. Intentional daily encounters with your spirit teach you to be aware and trusting of your inner voice. Learn to listen and hear your truest self—your spirit. It's not your gut speaking. Make it a habit to ask questions and seek direction for your life. A couple of my go-to questions are: What am I supposed to deposit and receive from the universe today? To whom and how am I to serve as a blessing?

3. Why do you want to have a connection with something greater than yourself? We go to the gym to be more fit; we eat more nutritiously to lose weight or to be healthier; we use aromatherapy to lower stress. What is your why—greater happiness, increased faith, healing—as it relates to spirituality? Knowing the reason you desire to be more spiritually tuned in is the best guide for building your own sacred practice.

17

PRAYER CHANGES THINGS

- What does the phrase "say your prayers" mean to you?

- How does prayer fit into your everyday life?

Pray on it. Pray over it.
Pray through it.

—Joanna Beck

After finishing our medical school interviews, my friends and I breathed a great sigh of relief and got into the car to travel several hours back to campus. I remember the sun was shining brightly, and the cool, crisp air lifted our spirits. The weather wasn't problematic, and we were looking forward to a relaxing, uneventful drive without delays. That's why we were caught completely off guard when the car spun out of control, crossing all lanes of the highway. As the car whirled, the only sounds I heard were echoes of prayers, even from the person who was an atheist.

In the midst of what seemed like a certain, fatal tragedy, everything stood still, as if someone had reached down and just stopped the spinning. Remarkably, we hadn't collided with anything or anyone, and oddly, there wasn't even a car near us. When the turning stopped, in one synchronized voice, almost sounding rehearsed, we all said, "Thank you, God."

The rest of the trip was uncannily quiet. No more than a few words were spoken. In that car, in that moment, each of us spun into a new relationship with prayer.

It's about spirituality, not religion

To put your mind at peace, this is not a Prescription on religion. Prayer is an option for everyone. I encourage you to find your own way while being inspired by my path and story. Hopefully, this offers you some reassurance to stay objective and keep an open heart.

I refer to prayer as the close, personal spiritual tie that offers day-to-day divine wisdom and hope. It is the union of faith, belief, and trust in the midst of vulnerability and pressing needs. Sometimes, it is simply an expression of gratitude.

Prayer acknowledges that there is an influence greater than you that is operating for the good of all humankind. My prayer life intimately connects me to a higher power. For me, it's God, but I respect that may not be the case for you. He knows my truth, and I patiently listen for His answer to my prayers while accepting that it may not always be what I desire. Besides, prayer isn't about getting your way; it's about sincerely trusting the presence of the Divine to be your light. It is also a constant reminder that I am not in this universe alone and, most importantly, that love and forgiveness are just a prayer away.

The more I embrace my prayer life, the healthier my decisions are. I feel more encouraged, and the quality of my life is more positively magnified. Prayer serves as a barrier between myself and the tough lessons of the world to protect and comfort me. It helps heal and bring about harmony. Prayer *really does* change things. It changes me and can change you.

Prayer is the ultimate practice of positive thinking

Prayer is positive reinforcement. Years ago, I had just landed in California from Ohio when I received a disturbing call. My brother had suffered a massive stroke. His condition looked grave, and the doctor encouraged me to get to the hospital as soon as possible. The news briefly incapacitated me, but the one thing I knew to do was to phone my pastor for prayer. I rushed through the airport to re-route and re-book my six-hour flight.

When I entered my brother's hospital room, he was on a ventilator; multiple bags of medicine and fluid were being administered. It looked grim. From my conversation with the medical staff, it was apparent they had given up. But to their surprise (because I am doctor), I held on to hope. I prayed. And I kept praying. With my whole heart and soul, I believed my brother would live and not die. I whispered into his ear that I would intercede for him—my family and I were steadfast in our petition to God. Within 48 hours, his kidney function returned, his blood pressure stabilized, and he was breathing on his own. A few days later, he was discharged from the hospital. Every nurse, physician, and staff member involved in his care called it a miracle. Little did they know, we had been praying for one.

Prayer keeps you moving forward

Prayer works! It may feel passive, but it's not. I have heard it stated that prayer is to the believer what breathing is to the body. When you pray, you are actively inviting and bringing about change in your life. A consistent prayer life lets you keep moving forward—during peak and valley experiences—with overflowing grace, mercy, and resilience. Prayer strengthens you to stand firm despite what the eyes see, the ears hear, and the mind thinks. Because you just *know* you'll get to the other side of your circumstances. There is power in the positivity of prayer.

Through prayer I discovered the will (divine plan and purpose) for my life—one that supersedes my best-laid plans. A will that edifies my soul, illuminates my path, directs my steps, and benefits more than just me.

When faced with a
crisis, do three things:
BREATHE,
PRAY,
and

Be Kind.

—Anne Lamott

PRESCRIPTION

For Changing Things with Prayer

17

Who's your closest friend? Reflect on how the relationship began and how it flourished into the loving friendship it is today.

Establishing a relationship with your higher power begins like any other meaningful connection. You start by getting to personally know the Divine Being by communicating through prayer. How?

1. *At first, set a time for prayer.* Eventually you'll be able to pray anytime and anywhere.

2. *Be thankful.* It's easy to complain, but you have to dig deeper to find gratitude. It can be as simple as being thankful for the rustling of the leaves or the softness of a snuggly blanket.

3. *Be authentic.* Talk from your heart. Prayers do not have to be eloquent or long. One of my most powerful prayers is "Please help."

4. *Listen more than you talk.* Prayer time is not about rambling off requests but a time to learn the plan for your life.

5. *Do not be frustrated with the "noes" and "not yets."* Believe your higher power knows best, because the Divine has access to the present and your future.

6. *Pray for others.* Expressing love for one another is showing love for the higher power.

7. *Keep a prayer journal* to be consistent in your prayer life, clear out distractions, and record how your prayers were answered.

As you spend time in prayer, you'll become familiar with your higher power's character, voice, and presence in your life. Ultimately, the bond between you will grow. How do I know? The most wonderful thing happened for me as my prayer life became stronger: God's omnipresence was palpable, and it felt very real and energizing.

Time to celebrate!

You did it! You've completed *all* Prescriptions that focus on healing! Take a moment to bask in your accomplishment. Take a moment to smile and feel the happiness. What will you do to celebrate? You've earned it! Now, take a moment to flip to the "Triumphs" section at the back of the book to write down a few things you're feeling good about in this achievement.

SCIENCE SAYS...

"Many patients expressed positive attitudes toward physician involvement in spiritual issues. Seventy-seven percent said physicians should consider patients' spiritual needs, 37 percent wanted their physicians to discuss religious beliefs with them more frequently, and 48 percent wanted their physicians to pray with them. However, 68 percent said their physician had never discussed religious beliefs with them."

—D. E. King and B. Bushwick.
"Beliefs and attitudes of hospital inpatients about faith, healing, and prayer," *Journal of Family Practice*, 994, October; 39(4): 349–52

Health

18

FOODS
AND MOODS

- Do you turn to food for some comfort?

- Do you frequently eat when you are not
  physically hungry?

Gluttony is an emotional escape,
a sign something is eating us.

—Peter De Vries

I stood motionless—as though taking even a shallow breath would trigger an alarm—staring at the scale as it caught my eye like a billboard when the number flashed over 300 pounds! A barrage of questions flooded my thoughts. How on earth had this happened? How did I become morbidly obese (as if just being obese wasn't enough)? How had a knife and fork turned into weapons of mass destruction? When did a pint of butter pecan Häagen-Dazs ice cream become my emotional support? What was eating a large extra-cheese pizza in a single serving trying to tell me? This entanglement had nothing to do with bad carbs, processed foods, and portion sizes. *I wasn't struggling with willpower and food choices. I was wrestling with deep unresolved pain.*

There isn't enough food in the world to even begin to comfort hurt. I tried to eat my way through the disappointments, but I couldn't.

What are you craving?

Potato chips or chocolate? Or are you trying to satisfy something other than a sweet or savory tooth? It's so darn easy to turn to food to console, avoid, and suppress feelings. Getting to the core of what you're attempting to hush up with a thick slice of red velvet cake or a plate of french fries is the first step toward regaining control of not only what you eat but also how you live. Until you do, you'll always make room in your belly—even when there is none—for another bite. Overeating has less to do with food and more to do with not wanting to experience discomforts—who does?—and triggers:

- Worries and anxiety
- Sadness and loneliness
- Frustrations
- Fears and stress
- Uncomfortable emotions
- Trauma

If you want to sever ties with binge eating, night cravings, and feeding emotional pangs, you have to unmask the hard stuff you don't want to deal with—food won't solve the problems.

An unhealthy coping mechanism

At best, overindulgence is an unhealthy coping mechanism—one that eventually stops doing the trick. At some point, eating a sleeve of cookies didn't make me feel any better than having two; actually, I felt worse. Overeating won't control a perpetual emotional hunger that is starving for your attention. The compulsive urge to stuff your face is a tip-off that your relationship with food has taken a sour turn and there's *something* you need to work through—it won't go away on its own.

Signs of an emotional eater

- *You eat more when exposed to stress.* Is it unforgiveness, loss, disappointment, loneliness, molestation, single-ness? Name the emotional unrest you are trying to lift with your fork. Many times, I found myself chewing on candy corn and peanuts after an overwhelming day at work, or eating more than one slice of cheesecake because it seemed easier than confronting my feelings. Food was my outlet to take the edge off the situation—until it didn't.

- *You eat mindlessly and when you are not physically hungry.* Have you ever found yourself standing in the kitchen scavenging through the refrigerator or cabinets shortly after finishing a meal? You don't even taste the food because your taste buds have tired out; it happens after large amounts of food. You know good and well you aren't hungry; you just have some unsettled emotions to feed.

- *You crave specific foods to feed your emotions.* As I mentioned earlier, my favorite was ice cream. Whatever was wrong seemed to get a little better with each spoonful of butter pecan ice cream. Unfortunately for me, ice cream couldn't chill my emotions once and for all. They kept coming back.

- *You feel guilty about eating.* Mostly, my guilt came after the food was gone, not while eating. I thought, *I can't believe I ate that entire bag of chips.* Ironically, I comforted my guilt by starting on the cupcakes next. In moments like this, you're frustrated about your relationship with food but feel unable to end it.

Healing from emotional eating

1. *Acknowledge your emotions.* It may be uncomfortable, but permit yourself to feel the emotion, to understand the source, and to heal. In other words, take the power

away from food by finding the strength, courage, and grit to deal with the pain. It's okay to shed tears. Journaling helps identify the let-down and opens a space to establish a plan to address the true problem instead of suppressing it with food—it won't work anyhow.

2. *Forgive yourself and others.* It happened and it hurt, but unforgiveness hurts too, and it mostly hurts you. Release it and nurture a healthier, happier, more harmonized you. Begin by connecting with your spirituality through prayer, creating a sacred time to be still, hearing and listening to your inner being, and exploring the power of your breath. Remember all that work you did in earlier Prescriptions? This is a good opportunity to refer back to those, if needed.

Adopt healthy lifestyle interventions

Find new ways to clear your head. Simple things like being more physically active, practicing meditation or relaxation techniques, and starting a hobby are great ways to replace emotional eating with new habits that make you feel better and feed your soul.

- *Be aware of emotional triggers.* Try not to leave yourself vulnerable to making poor choices. When possible, limit exposure to those things that set your fork in motion. If the trigger cannot be avoided, use your social circle for encouragement during times of high stress.

- *Keep temptations to a minimum.* Safe-proof your environment, much like parents do to prevent young children from harming themselves. Stock up on healthier food options to decrease grazing, which can lead to emotional eating. A carrot usually isn't the feel-good food you are looking for, but if it's the only option, you'll eat it instead of a bag of chips.

Overeating transiently dulls life's blows; facing the "real weight" you're carrying has a lasting transformation on your mind, body, and soul.

There is never
enough food
for the hungry

soul.

—**Dr. Gabriel Cousens**

PRESCRIPTION

For Why We Overeat

In *Writing to Heal*, Dr. James Pennebaker states, "The evidence is mounting that the act of writing about traumatic experience for as little as fifteen or twenty minutes a day for three or four days can produce measurable changes in physical and mental health. . . . Writing does more than affect your mental and physical health. You may start acting differently." How awesome is that?

To move in the direction of freedom from overeating and a strained relationship with food:

1.   For one week (by all means, continue the process as long as you need), set aside 20 minutes daily to journal about one trigger that causes you to overeat. Do not be hampered by trying to over-analyze each situation. You're simply heightening your awareness of a dysfunctional

coping mechanism and providing yourself with a safe place, a place where food is not a distraction from what's really bothering you, to sort out your feelings.

2. When you're triggered to overeat by a specific trauma or unpleasant memory you wrote about, go back to your journal and continue writing. Each time, take a deeper dive. Repeat this until the emotional discomfort no longer precipitates eating your feelings without thinking. The purpose is to generate a pause to allow you to choose an alternative coping technique.

3. It's helpful for you to know your objective for eating. What are you equating food with: love, comfort, companionship, reward, punishment, avoidance, denial?

4. Old habits are hard to break, so be prepared not to cave in and eat. How? Plan ahead. What are three healthy lifestyle tools (e.g., meditation, yoga, fitness, art therapy) you can use to avoid sticking a fork into your emotions? *Before* self-soothing with food, try one of the tools you listed.

SCIENCE SAYS...

"Thirty-eight percent of adults report they over-ate or ate unhealthy foods in the past month because of stress (half of these say they do it every week or even more frequently)."

—American Psychological Association. *Stress and Eating.* January 1, 2013. apa.org/news/press/releases/stress/2013/eating

19

GET TO THE ROOT OF YOUR HEALTH

- Do you know your family's health history?

- What's in your family tree that should be shared with your doctor?

We all carry inside of us people who came before us.

—Liam Callahan

Although there is some truth to the phrase "The apple doesn't fall far from the tree," DNA is not the be-all and end-all when it comes to your health. It is an alert that you may be in harm's way of specific diseases and illnesses. However, genetics as well as how you treat your body influence your health, and you have the last say on the latter. Bearing this in mind, your health is *your* personal matter. It's up to *you* to protect it. You don't have to become a victim of bad genes.

Like with most things, knowledge is king. Your family history tells a very key part of your story, so knowing it—ask and keep asking until the health secrets are out of the bag—can be the difference between life and death, sickness and health. Discovering your roots lets you take part in painting your own wellness portrait. It's also vital to ending cycles of poor health and building a healthy legacy for generations to come.

Get to the roots of your family tree

Members of the same pedigree have a lot of commonalities in their physical and mental health. So when you are getting up to speed on family affairs, asking for your auntie's secret recipe, or reminiscing over a photo of Grandpa standing in front of his beloved pickup truck (one of my only pictures of my grandfather), you *must* remember to ask about your family's medical history.

Ask questions *and* document the answers; don't be deterred by awkwardness. Nudge the unhealthy skeletons out of the closet. Start with the big picture, and get as many details as you can from your loved ones.

- What patterns of disorders are a part of the family linage? The more generations an illness occurs, the more at risk you are.

- What age were family members when diagnosed with a specific condition? The younger they were, the more likely ancestry was involved.

- What was the specific cause of death? This information can help sort out a lot about the health of the family. Obituaries and death certificates can fill in the holes.

Being informed can be the gift that keeps on giving. Giving life, that is!

Knowing is half the battle

As a physician, I've woefully had to deliver fatal diagnoses after diseases silently progressed to advanced stages. No one is an island unto themselves. A little investigative legwork on your biological tree may lead to earlier detection and treatment—and possibly entirely sidestepping a poor prognosis. You've heard it before, but it bears repeating: "An ounce of prevention is worth a pound of cure." It's always best to avoid a problem than try to fix it.

For example, dementia, asthma, cancer, high blood pressure, diabetes, depression, and schizophrenia are health conditions that tend to run in families. Your doctor can use this as a guide to screen you for potential illnesses. If someone in your immediate bloodline had breast cancer at the age of 40, for instance, mammograms for descendants would start at age 30 instead of 40. Since it is a consensus that prevention is better than cure, knowing your family details is half your health battle.

Knowing doesn't etch your fate in stone

What you don't know *can* hurt you, and it can also hurt your children! My advice? Dig three generations deep. Parents may have genes that do not show up in either of them, but when two people with recessive (unexpressed) genes have a child, the child can express the condition. It can be lovely to be surprised with a blue-eyed child, but it would be better to be forewarned about the possibility of cystic fibrosis or sickle cell anemia.

Having a predisposition for a particular illness does not etch your fate in stone. In fact, due to tremendous advances in health care, if intervention is timely, your chances of beating the odds are much improved from those of your ancestors. Heart disease has shortened the lives of several of my family members. My father died from multivessel heart disease. This awareness is at the center of my approach to nutrition, fitness, and stress management. It is also the push behind monitoring my cholesterol and blood pressure. Because of my family history, I do my part to reduce my risk of heart disease. Ignorance isn't bliss. Knowledge is power!

No one should be a sitting duck

If you are adopted or have adopted children, companies like 23andMe can be instrumental in getting to the roots of your health, which, if I haven't made it obvious by now, could be lifesaving. Thank goodness, no one has to be a sitting duck.

The preservation of
health is easier than
the cure of

disease.

—B. J. Palmer

PRESCRIPTION

For Getting to the Roots of Your Health

Sadly, when it comes to the state of your health, family members end up suffering from the same conditions over and over again, partly due to lack of knowledge about their family medical history. It doesn't have to be that way. And it shouldn't be. To break the cycle of ill-health, collect a near-complete family history. Knowing *something* is better than knowing nothing. And remember, swim three generations back in the gene pool, if possible. Use this list to get started.

1. Find out about diseases identified in more than one close relative.
2. Get the details: Who had the disease, the age it was diagnosed, what were the symptoms, how was it treated, and cause of death (it's usually a complication of the illness).

3. Write down illnesses that occurred in relatives at young ages.
4. Inquire of health issues that are rare in a particular gender, such as breast cancer in a male.
5. Make note of any serious conditions like cancers, dementia, strokes, and heart attacks.
6. Record long-term health conditions such as high blood pressure, high cholesterol, asthma, and kidney disease.
7. Research combinations of illnesses within the family; for instance, breast and ovarian cancer or heart disease and diabetes.
8. Ask about a family history of mental problems.
9. If there are any documents related to medical conditions or deaths, keep a copy.
10. Learn about your family's ancestry. It can be fun and informative to discover from which countries your relatives descended.

Once you know, pass along the knowledge to your doctor and other family members, then use it to make better lifestyle choices. "My Family Health Portrait" is a great tool for saving and updating your family's medical history. Visit the site at phgkb.cdc.gov/FHH/html/index.html. We don't want all your hard detective work to get misplaced. Another perk of using the site is that you'll be the focus of the discussions, this time for a positive reason, by downloading the health profile and creating a family newsletter or postcard. A healthy win for you and your family!

You deserve a pat on the back for taking on this Prescription, so give yourself one—now. It can be scary and exhausting to dig into your roots. Congratulations on stocking up on powerful health knowledge!

20

TAKE YOUR HEALTH CARE PERSONALLY

- When was your last annual physical exam?

- How do you tailor doctor visits to address the mind-body-spirit?

An ounce of prevention is worth
a pound of cure.

—Benjamin Franklin

"One-size-fits-all" seldom applies, and there's certainly no one approach to health care for everyone. Such a generic strategy assumes that all things are created equal and ignores our uniqueness. Age, gender, culture, sexual orientation, religion, socioeconomic factors, and family and personal history are key parts of the bigger health and wellness picture. Since no two people are exactly alike, it stands to reason that their health needs aren't identical either. Consequently, patient-tailored health care is the only way to deliver the right care to the right person—to you.

How do you customize your health?
The quick-and-dirty answer is to make it specifically about you—define what health and wellness looks and feels like to you against the backdrop of your risk factors. After all, your health care should offer the right solutions to energize all aspects of *your* life. So how do you make your health more personal and less generic?

- Open up the conversation with your doctor to more than body aches, blood pressure, and weight.
- Speak up about mental stress, changes in libido, and unhealthy habits.
- Be honest about your challenges, and ask for options.
- Share your dietary, spiritual, and end-of-life preferences.
- Discuss the support and resources available to meet your needs.
- Set measurable health goals with specific actions to achieve them.

- Go off script; be candid about traumas from drug addiction to childhood molestation to being in loveless marriages. Don't keep secrets.

You should feel safe to talk with your health-care provider about sensitive issues impacting your mental and spiritual well-being because, ultimately, they will impact your physical health too. If there is apprehension in the room or you don't feel you connect well, then feel comfortable finding a new health-care provider. It's imperative that you are not dismissed, that your health concerns are not ignored.

A guide to a conversation about your personal health

So what should you expect at a doctor's appointment, and what are the most healthful topics to discuss? Start with the basics and then ease into specifics about yourself. Below are guides according to approximate age. Find yours and observe how it evolves through the years.

In your 20s (20 and terrific)

- Discuss testing for sexually transmitted diseases, including HIV.
- Check your vaccination status, including the meningococcal vaccine.
- Set social media parameters.
- Address healthy nutrition and exercise.
- *Women:* A pap smear is recommended every three years, starting at age 21. Consider testing for human

papillomavirus (HPV); the goal is to be "one fewer" person with cervical cancer.

- *Men:* You'll need to drop your pants too. A testicular exam detects abnormalities in the testicles.

Be specific about:

- Are you in an abusive (physically, mentally, or sexually) relationship?
- Have you been molested or raped?
- Are you struggling with depression, anxiety, attention deficit disorder, or suicide?
- Do you binge drink alcohol or use drugs or nicotine?
- Are you participating in any impulsive behaviors (unprotected sex, drinking and driving)?
- Do you have any unhealthy eating behaviors (anorexia, bulimia)?
- Discuss your sexual orientation.

In your 30s (30 and thriving)

- Speak with your doctor regarding changes in your health and weight.
- *Women:* Ask about your risk of breast cancer. (It's much less common, but men can ask this question too.)
- *Women:* If your pap smear is combined with HPV testing and you've had normal results, testing can now be performed every five years, unless you have risk factors for cervical cancer; otherwise, as recommended.

Be specific about:

- Any of the topics listed under the 20s are fair game.
- If you have children, be open about the woes of managing parenthood.
- What are your struggles as an adult?
- How do you heal from personal trauma?

In your 40s (40 and fantastic)

- News flash: You are due for a colonoscopy. Isn't it nice that you no longer need to wait until you turn 50? There is some good news: You will not need to repeat the procedure for 3 to 10 years, depending on the findings. But getting it done is necessary, because colon cancer is the third most common cancer diagnosed in Americans.
- Do not be shy—talk with your doctor about your sexual health (decreased libido, erectile dysfunction).
- Stop squinting, and have your vision tested. If you are over 45, checking for glaucoma is a good idea.
- An EKG may be in order, depending upon your risk for heart disease.
- *Women:* Ladies, take a deep breath and put them on the mammography machine. A yearly mammogram is *necessary*, not optional. Breast cancer is one of the leading cancers diagnosed in American women.
- *Women:* Beginning at age 45, blood tests for high cholesterol in women at increased risk for coronary heart disease and for diabetes are part of the annual physical.

- *Men:* Do not sigh. The gloves are on, and it is time for a digital check of the prostate—it'll be quick.

Be specific about:

- How to establish work-life harmony?
- What are some tools to manage life stress?
- Ways to improve quality of sleep?
- How to increase personal happiness?

In your 50s (50 and fabulous)

- Everybody roll up your sleeve for a shingles vaccine.
- *Women:* Turn down the heat! Hot flashes, night sweats, mood swings, and vaginal dryness—if it has been one year since your last period, it's probably *menopause*. Discuss your treatment options. If there is a personal or family history of breast cancer or heart disease, hormone therapy may not be the right choice.

Be specific about:

- What are your fears about aging?
- Are you experiencing mild forgetfulness?
- If you have children, how do you handle the empty-nest syndrome?
- Are body changes such as sagging skin, weight gain, drooping breasts, and graying hair causing a self-esteem crisis?
- Do you have concerns about being divorced and dating again?

In your 60s (60 and still sexy)

- Oh, those bones! Ask your doctor about a bone density test. Also, fall-proof your home. A fall could result in a hip fracture and land you in a rehabilitation facility.
- Get your pneumonia vaccine.
- Have your hearing tested, even if you may be benefiting from selective hearing.
- If you have a smoking history, talk to your doctor about an ultrasound to screen for an abdominal aortic aneurysm.
- *Women:* Pap smears can be discontinued in women over 65 with no risk factors for cervical cancer, or women who have had a hysterectomy for reasons other than cancer.

Be specific about:
- Are you feeling alone?
- Any worries about who will help you if your health fails?
- How do stay mentally sharp and physically independent?
- Should you retire, and what's next if you do?

In your 70s (70 and sassy)

- I can't emphasize this enough: Stay steady on your feet. It may be a good idea to get a referral to physical therapy for fall prevention.
- Sexually transmitted infections aren't reserved for the young and free. Discuss your sexual health and whether you should have testing.

- To avoid depression setting in, talk with your doctor about the blues due to loss of loved ones and friends and not being able to do the things you once could.
- Appoint someone to have the last say when you can no longer express your wishes.
- If you live alone, have a plan to signal for help. Consider a medical alert device.

Be specific about:

- Is it safe to continue living in your own home?
- Are you noticing a progressive decline in your memory?
- Do you need help shopping, cleaning, cooking, bathing, banking, or dressing?
- How do you stay physically active?

Don't take a passive role

"If it's not personal, don't take it personally." This is a great rule to live by, but it does not apply to your health—living well is *always* personal. After the standard medical boxes have been checked off, push to carve out a more individualized and interactive game plan for your health. Because it can be easy to take a passive role, heed my expert advice: *Don't be passive.* Remember, *you have the expertise and experience of knowing your body, and your particular needs, better than anyone.* Prepare and respectfully chime in to tailor the visit to you. It will be most rewarding for both you and your physician!

"

Your health is what
you make of it.
Everything you do and
think either adds to
the vitality,
energy and spirit
you possess or
takes away

 from it.

—**Ann Wigmore**

"

PRESCRIPTION

For Taking Your Health Care Personally

Ready to take a more personal approach to your health? It'll ensure your care is targeted to fit you, specifically. My advice for you is to speak up. Don't be hush-hush about what is really bothering you—withholding it can be a physical or mental health risk.

I hesitate to make this next suggestion because I've heard a lot of sighs over the years, but here it is: Keep a health journal. Yes, another journal—having your own little library of journals is a safe place to record and process how life is affecting you mentally, spiritually, and physically. In your health journal, jot down concerns (along with the details) you would like to discuss with your physician. If you find an issue embarrassing or not so pleasant to bring up, ask the medical assistant to make a copy of your notes to give to the doctor.

Here is a framework to support having an open dialogue with your health provider:

1. What exactly is the issue? No need to beat around the bush; just say it. Be up front about any cultural or personal sensitivities surrounding the problem. For example, lead with "This is a difficult topic for me to talk about because . . ."

2. When did the [insert your concern] occur?

3. Why are you talking about it now?

4. What effect is the problem having on your well-being?

5. What would make the situation better for you?

6. What *specifically* can the doctor do to help (a referral, support group, information)? No one can read your mind.

7. Be honest about personal habits in order to receive the best care and medical advice. Believe me, there isn't much we haven't heard.

The doctor's office is a no-judgment, private zone. Have you heard of the Health Insurance Portability and Accountability Act (HIPAA)? All that fancy language to explain that sensitive, patient-health information is protected from being disclosed without the patient's consent or knowledge. Take advantage of it to get everything off your chest.

21
RAISE YOUR NUTRITIONAL IQ

- What is your nutritional IQ?

- Are you getting all the nutrition you need?

> The definition of insanity is doing the same thing over and over again but expecting different results.
>
> **—Albert Einstein**

When people hear that I've dropped 140 pounds, they tend to blurt out, *"How?"* The curiosity is almost palpable! *Is this the magic solution?* Is it for me? Well, if you are in search of a quick fix, my journey wasn't quick. I know that can feel like a bit of a deflation for some.

Most people want to hear what I did, but let me tell you what I *didn't* do. I *did not* starve myself, use fad diets, or spend countless hours in a gym. And while I have yo-yo dieted more times than I care to admit (and actually lost weight), I always returned to my old eating habits and put the weight right back on—and, in many cases, even a few extra pounds on top of that! I've had so many different-size clothes in my closet, I could have opened a boutique. And then I realized: *Dieting doesn't work for me.* I don't know how many diets I tried before finally realizing that. So many that I proved Albert Einstein's definition of insanity was correct—not my original intention!

Get the facts

Let's boil it down to the cold, hard facts. You already know this, yet you (like I did) keep holding out hope that there is a magic solution. *But there isn't.* There are no shortcuts for healthy eating. Many advertisements, however, will try and sell you one—that's where the money is. But deep down, we know better, don't we? So do not be swayed. Not only are those quick fixes dangerous, but they won't work long term. Getting the facts about foods and improving your nutritional IQ is not only the best way to lose weight but also the ideal plan for *keeping the weight off.* Remember what I said about my closet? After giving up on finding an overnight solution, I'm happy to report that I lost those 140 pounds and have kept them off for several years.

Beef up your nutritional IQ

Food is not the enemy. Let go of that negativity. The more you improve your nutritional IQ, you'll discover you have plenty of food options and will therefore have a more positive relationship with food, especially once you learn a thing or two about how to combine foods and not gorge yourself on carbs.

Before taking medicine, most people ask: *What is the medication, why is it being prescribed, and what are the potential side effects?* Exercising that same level of concern when eating could sway you toward food selections that contribute to your well-being and not compromise it. Put simply, think before you eat, and do not be misled by your eyes.

Carbs

Carbohydrates have taken a lot of heat, and their reputation has been tarnished. They're your main source of energy. If you don't want to run out of steam, you need them; however, when it comes to carbohydrates, it's complex—vegetables, whole grains, beans, and lentils—not simple. Complex carbs cause a lower rise in blood sugar. It's the simple carbs—cookies, candy, fruit juice, most cereal—that literally tip the scale. A moment on your lips can seem to become a lifetime on your hips. Complex carbohydrates should be 45 to 65 percent of your total daily calories, so you don't have to eat carb-free, just carb-smart.

When I was faced with my own elevated blood sugar, homing in on my knowledge of carbs made all the difference—the difference between my becoming a diabetic or not. Balancing carbohydrates reversed my blood sugar from something quite scary to something normal. Maybe there is some truth in the adage "Who eats well feels well."

Protein

High-protein diets are all the rave! Protein is the chief muscle food, but a bigger burger doesn't equal bigger muscles. Rather than restricting your spread to as many proteins as you can eat, selecting protein from better sources is likely what your diet is craving. Fish, poultry, beans, nuts, and whole grains give you the most nutritional bang minus extra fat. Also try some plant-based proteins. Have you ever had black bean tacos? Delicious! Too much of a good thing, even protein, can be a not-so-good thing, leading to kidney disease, dehydration, or high cholesterol. It's all about balance.

Veggies

It's not a rule just for kids. Adults shouldn't leave the table without eating all their vegetables either. They really are nature's vitamins and minerals—refer to the Prescription on supplements and nutrients. Veggies supply your body with vitamin C, folate, potassium, and more. Five servings of fruit and vegetables a day can aid in preventing heart disease and some cancers.

Fats

Some fats are healthier than others, but don't use this as an excuse to be heavy-handed with healthy fats. On average, six teaspoons of oil a day is enough, including the fat already in foods. Oils that are liquid at room temperature, such as those in nuts and avocados, make a more favorable imprint on your heart.

Also, some oils lose their healthy properties at high heats, so learn the smoke point—where the fats start to break down and release free radicals—for the oil of your choice. There's nothing good about a healthy fat gone rogue.

Calcium and vitamin D

Sorry to break the news, but ice cream doesn't satisfy the recommendations for calcium and vitamin D—oh, how I wish! And the verdict isn't final on whether dairy is in or out, though it is unanimous that your bones need calcium and vitamin D to be strong and keep you on your feet. That said, you may find it helpful to know that there's calcium beyond the dairy aisle—spinach, kale, edamame, almonds, dried figs (but not fig cookies). Depending on your age and gender, 1200 mg to 1500 mg of calcium and 600 IU to 800 IU of vitamin D per day is recommended to reduce the risk of osteoporosis, improve bone density, and decrease the risk of adult bone fractures with falls. The more you know about what you eat, the more you'll be able to eat yourself to healing, health, and happiness one bite at a time!

One cannot think well,
love well,
sleep well,
if one has not

dined well.

—Virginia Woolf

PRESCRIPTION

For Raising Your Nutritional IQ

Fat-free, sugar-free, taste-free foods are a setup for binge eating. Think of (and reach for) nutritional, weight-friendly, delicious options instead of deprivation. It's really about eating a harmony of healthy foods as well as your favorite flavors.

To be sure we're on the same plate, use your favorite foods to create a meal-and-snack plan for a week. As a general rule, snacks should be less than 200 calories. Having second thoughts about that 400-calorie frozen drink? For your meals, select a food from each category. You are not limited to the foods listed below; they are only examples.

1. Complex carbs: quinoa, whole grains, lentils, sweet potatoes, butternut squash, brown rice
2. Simple carbs: sweetened breakfast cereals, bread, fruit, sweets, wine

3. Lean protein: salmon, tofu, poultry, beans, Greek yogurt, eggs

4. Fats: nuts, avocado, peanut butter, dark chocolate, olive oil

5. Calcium + vitamin D: milk, cottage cheese, broccoli, canned tuna, wild mushrooms

For example, my favorite breakfast is a veggie sausage patty (lean protein) and steel oats (complex carbs) made with almond milk (calcium and vitamin D), blueberries (simple carbs), and walnuts (fat). I'm fueled to start the day!

My go-to snack is popcorn, which is a whole grain. That means it has complex carbs and fiber. Win-win! A well-developed nutritional palate is the new wellness.

Time to celebrate!

Consider this a *HOORAY* moment! These pauses to celebrate are built in to remind you to stay positive and to support you in becoming your own best fan. They also give you a reference point to value your achievements and stick-to-it ability. Toot your horn in the "Triumph" pages about how a more gratifying life is starting to take shape.

SCIENCE SAYS...

"71% of the public thinks granola bars are healthy, while only 28% of the hundreds of nutritionists surveyed agreed with that assessment."

—2016 poll conducted by the *New York Times*

22

MOVE, REACH, AND STRETCH

- Do you prefer to sit or stand?

- Besides exercise, what movements are part of your daily routine?

> The body will become better at whatever you do, or don't do. You don't move? The body will make you better at NOT moving. If you move, your body will allow more movement.
>
> **—Ido Portal**

Sit down. Stay put. And don't move. Not so fast (you know what I mean). As humans, we are not meant to be sedentary. Browsing, scrolling, and surfing are misnomers (sounds like you're moving; you're not)—reaching for the remote or tapping on a computer screen or keyboard is not being active. Our bones, joints, muscles, ligaments, and tendons work in synchrony to create motions—walk, run, leap, dance, play, bend, stretch, squat—that help perform activities of daily living. All the more reason not to choose to be a bump on a log.

We're designed to be fluid and keep moving. Movement is an expression of vitality and connectedness between the mind and body. The more we gravitate toward the nearest seat, the more we lose that mind-body connection.

Put your body in motion

Movement is more dynamic and broader than exercise—they are not one in the same. You might be able to slip by without exercising (not a good idea), but that's not true of movement. If you don't move it, you lose it—functionality and flexibility. This by no means depreciates the immense value of fitness. On the other hand, don't let an hour workout take you out of action for the rest of the day. The goal of movement is not to burn calories or to define your physique. When you put your body in motion, it *frees you* from restrictions and *empowers you* to flow into your larger purpose. Movement provides the strength, agility, endurance, and balance to express yourself in every dimension of your life.

Move with intention

Mindful movements engage the whole body and whole mind. This is what attracted me to the Gyrotonic Method, which combines rotations and spiral movements with to enlarge your expansion and improve your stability. I can hear Keelie, my former instructor, telling me to reach through the top of my head, fingers, and toes to experience the full range of motion of every joint (sometimes she had to push me a tiny bit, sometimes a lot). Moving more efficiently in every way has also been a huge benefit of my Pilates class. I credit Mary and Julie (my other instructors) for teaching me to stretch toward life while gliding on a reformer platform with resistance to build core strength and muscle balance.

Healthy movements don't have to be complex. They can be performed from the comfort of your home or workspace, without getting sweaty or changing into gym clothes. Start with the basics, stand up after sitting for an hour. Take the stairs. Replace your chair with an exercise ball. Get up and go get whatever you may need. Take advantage of every opportunity to make a move.

Adapt and adjust your movements

Like real life, holistic movement includes self-awareness and adjustments to accommodate what is going on in the present moment. Do not force it. Respect your body. Listen and adapt to environmental and emotional clues. What is your body communicating to you? Sometimes mine wants a stretch, other times it desires a walk; maybe my body longs for more vigorous movement, and then there are times when it just needs to dance! When you move in a supportive way, it is a life hack to combat fatigue, restlessness, depression, pain, aging poorly, and some health problems.

Movement is an act of self-love

Being able to move freely is an entry for your gratitude journal. Movement should feel like love, like joy. It is being kind to your body. It's honoring all that your body can do and does to support your life. Don't get distracted by what your body looks like. If that's a bit of a struggle for you, focus on just one thing you appreciate about your body, and let love grow from there. Because every body, regardless of shape, size, or color, is a beautiful body—anyone or anything that says differently isn't telling the truth. Movement is a muse to inspire you to feel good about, be good to, and love the body you are in.

Movement is your
nature and your
birthright. You need
a lot of it to thrive
and bring out
your happy . . .
just like when
you were a

kid.

—Courtney Towny

PRESCRIPTION

For Moving, Reaching, and Stretching

Don't just sit there. Heaven forbid you have to get back up once you've already sat down, but if you do, you should be thankful. Don't sigh about it. Unless that sigh is a deep, cleansing breath you take before moving, because that is exactly what I want you to do. After sitting for an hour, take a breath, give the chair a break, and exercise your freedom to move. Here are some ways to get you moving:

1. Walk to a restaurant for lunch, or bring your lunch and walk around your office.
2. Set an alert to stand up and stretch.
3. Opt for the stairs.
4. Make multiple trips. You don't have carry all the groceries in the house in one trip to avoid walking back to the car.

5. If you can do it standing, stand.

6. Put on some feel-good music and dance around the house.

Don't put off what you can do right now. Let's S—T—R—E—T—C—H.

- Stand tall with your back and neck straight, as if you have a string attached to the top of your head and someone is gently tugging on it.

- Place your feet hip-width apart with your arms extended overhead.

- Release the tightness in your neck, shoulders, triceps, and back.

- Bend the right elbow so that your right palm lies on your upper back.

- Reach your left hand over to grasp just below the right elbow.

- Gently pull your elbow down and back.

- Hold the stretch for about 45 seconds.

- Switch arms and repeat.

Feel your blood flow to awaken and elongate each muscle. As your body relaxes and becomes more flexible, notice as the tension leaves the muscle. Do this stretch daily; it is good for the body and mind.

23

FITNESS IS A LIFESTYLE

- Do you have a regular workout schedule?

- What obstacles interfere with keeping weekly workout hours?

Fitness isn't a seasonal hobby.
Fitness is a lifestyle.

—Unknown

Again, exercise and movement are not one and the same. In the interest of clarity, make sure you've read the "For Moving, Reaching, and Stretching" Prescription before challenging yourself to make fitness a lifestyle.

It's undeniable that fitness is good for your health and that you should aim to do some form of it on more days than not, but it's not always easy to stay on track. You set goals and resolutions, maybe even team up with others with similar intentions. You start off strong, and then it tapers off. But that's to be expected, especially when you aren't a person who works out regularly. Exercise must be more than a trend or a hobby to not slip from consistency to an occasional gym stop. If you want to see your body transform, exercise has to be as automatic as breathing, eating, and sleeping.

Remember your mission

Why do you want to feel the burn? We've all experienced an on-again, off-again, back-on-again, back-off-again relationship with exercise. But that roller-coaster ride isn't going to produce the results we want; even if it does, it certainly won't maintain them. Reminding myself of what motivated me to create a goal or mission makes a significant difference in my endurance; that's also true when it comes to exercise. You need a personal connection to your *why*. For me, I don't want to be offered the seat belt extender again, and I don't want to recommend something to my patients that I am not willing to do. Working out because it's good for you and because you should do it works for some, but not everybody. Being deliberate about what you want to achieve—reduce stress, fit into that dress, improve your health—keeps you focused even when you would rather skip the gym. It also helps you do something you enjoy so that it doesn't feel like another dreaded task, eating away at your time.

Routine, routine, routine

Don't let life get between you and your workout. It's not always convenient, but both the major and subtle benefits of breaking a sweat are endless. However, they only come when working out is routine and not a 30-day challenge. I suggest you start small and build momentum rather than going big and ending up at home. As a rule of thumb, *something* definitely outweighs *nothing* when it comes to getting off the couch.

Sculpted biceps, triceps, pecs, and quads are just some of the rewards of a fitness habit. Exercise increases strength, improves balance and flexibility, sparks energy, and enhances mental clarity. It also helps regulate blood pressure and blood sugar and lower cholesterol. As an added perk, it boosts confidence and ends your exercise rut. If you're already a fitness enthusiast, keep up the good work. If not, it's never too late to become one. Routine physical activity is one of the secrets to a better quality of life and a better attitude.

Four pillars of fitness

In terms of exercise, confusion isn't a bad thing—muscle confusion, that is. While it is best to have a routine for *when* you work out, do not be a creature of habit when it comes to *what kind* of workout you do. Mixing up your regimen calls on different muscles, lessens the chances of your goals plateauing, and maximizes your efforts. If I had it my way, I'd prefer to cycle (spin class) my way to the most fit version of me. But after clipping into the bike pedals for a few years, it finally clicked that I was neglecting other areas of fitness and compromising my overall progress. There are four pillars of fitness, and each is important for a total mind-body makeover.

- Strength training
- Cardiovascular activity
- Balance exercises
- Joint flexibility

Find the right combination of lunges, squats, weight training, elliptical, and jogging to look better, feel better, and live longer and healthier.

The plan

Are you going for the bronze, silver, or gold? The basic fitness plan includes 150 minutes of moderately intense exercise a week. If 30 minutes for five days a week is a stretch given your schedule, do the math: $10 + 10 + 10 = 30$; $15 + 15 = 30$; $20 + 10 = 30$. Do you see where I'm going with this? Tailor your workout to meet your needs so that it doesn't throw your schedule completely out of whack. No matter how you choose to add up the time, a good exercise goal to work toward is to maintain your heart rate at a level where working out and having a conversation is possible but requires pauses so you can catch your breath.

Overall, a big plus for lacing up your sneakers is that just-worked-out feeling: You committed, you pushed your limits, you crushed it, and your future self will thank you!

Exercise not only
changes your body.
It changes your mind,
your attitude,
and your

mood.

—Unknown

PRESCRIPTION 23

For Making Fitness a Lifestyle

On average, it can take you more than 21 days to create a fitness habit. Keep pressing, and expect to experience some dips in your motivation. It happens. Just don't let a dip or two permanently stop you from exercising.

How do you push through the slumps when your inner couch potato is tempting you? To make fitness less about willpower and more about a decision, I crafted an anti-excuses pact: *On Your Mark, Get Set, Go Pre-commitment Strategy.* It's helps me to avoid procrastination or canceling my rendezvous with the gym. When you can't "just do it," devise a plan.

1. On Your Mark
   - Pack your gym bag in advance.
   - Check in with your workout partner (but be prepared to go it alone) and confirm a sitter if needed.

- Have a backup plan (in case of bad weather, the class is full, or your favorite machine is taken).
- Properly hydrate to sweat it out.
- Prepare a pre-workout snack to fuel the body for the best performance.

2. *Get Set* (each week)
   - Set the days (make exercise a priority).
   - Set the time (lock in your commitment).
   - Set the duration (it's not about long hours but what you do in the time you have).
   - Set the types of workouts (don't wing it).
   - Set the goals (have a game plan).

3. *Go*

It's all in the details. Log your fitness regimen to easily keep tabs on how you're shaping up. And yes, I've designed a Life in Harmony Fitness Log to share with you, but feel free to use a notebook or a workout app of your choice.

- Note how you felt before, during, and after working out (use an emoji). This gives you a snapshot of how exercise supports your mental well-being.
- List 30- and 90-day fitness goals and the importance of achieving them.
- Take progress pictures every month.
- Record improvements (weight, body measurements, stamina, muscle mass, nutrition).
- Chart your wellness by noting changes in your general health: blood pressure, diabetes, headaches, cholesterol, fibromyalgia.

- Choose short- and long-term rewards. Sometimes having a carrot dangling within reach can prevent you from derailing.
- Write down new workouts you want to try (e.g., skating, swimming, dancing, yoga, jump-roping, bicycling, hiking, weight training).

24

DON'T GIVE UP ON GIVING UP

- Do you use smoking or alcohol to relieve stress?

- What effect does smoking or drinking have on your life?

Smoking and drinking too much
is not the way to fitness.
Love your body and treat it good.

—Sunny Leone

You tell yourself you can quit if you really want to, so if you know it's bad for your health and shortens your life, why don't you really want to? You've even admitted to not liking it, hating the smell, or disapproving of how it changes your behavior. Yet you still do it. Calling it quits starts with understanding the reasons nicotine and alcohol are your significant others.

There's no need to blow smoke. Going tobacco-free and limiting alcoholic drinks require a lot of effort. If they were easy, this conversation and Prescription would not be necessary. It's not just about kicking the unhealthy habits of using addictive substances; it's also about modifying how you live and cope with life's stressors. If old age and sound health are goals, then putting out the cigarettes and cutting back on alcohol are non-negotiable. They're also very powerful health moves—and *it's never too late*.

Celebrate your independence by nixing dependence
There's more to the story. Before winding down with a glass of Pinot Noir under the pretense of protecting your heart, an overindulgence of red wine (or any alcohol for that matter) *increases* the risk of many health problems and can cancel out some of your positive lifestyle choices. For instance, you can eat clean the entire week and then render your efforts null and void by binge drinking on the weekend, because heavy drinking obstructs the body's ability to absorb nutrients. By the way, you don't have to be an alcoholic to suffer the unwelcome side effects of too much alcohol consumption.

People have all kinds of justifications for drinking heavily: to relieve stress, to decrease social inhibitions, to cope with mental illnesses, to have fun, and so on. I don't disagree that people can experience a temporary reprieve; however, even that benefit self-destructs. The road ahead becomes darker when alcohol is the coping mechanism. It is paved with depression (more than half of suicides are linked to alcohol), anxiety, risky behavior, and personality disorders.

If . . .

- your intuition tells you to cut back, or
- you've been told you need to cut back, or
- you avoid letting others know just how much you drink,

. . . those are cues that you should minimize your alcohol intake to reduce your risk of its damaging effects.

Too many spirits can put a real damper on your spirit. Don't be fooled into believing that you can eat and drink to your heart's content—unless your heart is content with one drink (for women), or one to two drinks (for men) in a sitting. Have a cocktail, spiked eggnog, or hot apple cider with rum in moderation. Too much of a good thing isn't healthy. If you have trouble stopping, it's best not to get started. Drinking problems can sneak up on you, but the consequences can quickly get out of hand and cause job loss, impaired memory, ruined relationships, poor judgement, dependence . . . the list is long.

The real skinny on cigarettes

Whew! Things have changed from the once-glamorized image of smoking to the unpleasant, frightening habit it's known to be today. In the past, a tall, sexy, slender woman holding a long, thin cigarette was marketed to imply, *If you smoke this you can look like this*. The unmasked truth? That once-glamorous gal is a frail woman wearing an oxygen mask, denoting smoking as the life-threatening habit it is. Today we know the real skinny—that filling your lungs with a thick cloud of smoke is anything but alluring.

It's not breaking news that smoking is harmful, but the "rule of seven" states that a person must hear or see something seven times before they act on it. Whether I need to repeat it 7 or 70 times, let this message sink in: Smoking is the number-one cause of preventable diseases, disabilities, and deaths in the United States. The key word is *preventable*—capable of being avoided.

Nonsmoker news

If you think you're in the clear because you do not smoke, think again. Are you familiar with secondhand smoke? It contains chemicals and toxins that can worsen preexisting conditions and cause cancer. An individual's "right" to smoke could be making those around them sick. And no, smoking outside or rolling down the car window doesn't filter out the noxious by-products of tobacco. Deep down, you know that!

The "C" word

Let's stop tiptoeing around the "C" word. Bringing up cancer is not a scare tactic. It cannot, unfortunately, be excluded from the real cost of smoking and excessive alcohol consumption. So ask yourself: Is a history of short-lived buzzes worth it? Although cancer is usually associated with smoking, alcohol is also a contributor to some cancers, such as those of the mouth, throat, stomach, and liver. What's guaranteed is that smoking cigarettes and drinking too much alcohol will affect your quality of life and jeopardize longevity, but the silver lining is that quitting at any time greatly slashes the hazards of these vices.

"

You leave old habits
behind by starting out
with the thought,
'I release the need
for this in my

life.'

—Dr. Wayne W. Dyer

PRESCRIPTION

For Not Giving Up on Giving Up

Whether it's overeating, overspending, overdrinking, or smoking, breaking up is hard to do. It is a test of mindset and patience. Before you take on the challenge, mentally prepare yourself:

- Start by exploring why you're doing what you're doing. In any situation, pinpointing the problem is necessary before you can find a solution. Being truthful with yourself about where the unhealthy habits are stemming from lets you put your finger on your triggers. Then you can work through underlying life events and establish favorable behaviors as an outlet to deal with them.

- Think about replacing negative activities from an optimistic perspective. You want to do more of what makes you feel good and less of what makes you feel bad.

Focusing on what you have to gain instead of what you are losing is much more encouraging. It can make you less likely to relapse—or at least cut back the number of times that you do.

These tips helped me prepare my own frame of mind as I geared up to address my overindulgence of food. Unhealthy behaviors do provide some gratification—eating comforted me—so instead of going cold turkey, I found equally satisfying substitutes. I'm no Picasso, but art therapy helped me put my fork down.

Don't give up on giving up. Stop nasty habits from destroying your life. If you don't smoke or drink excessively, answer the following questions based on your personal vices:

1. What triggers you to smoke or drink? Be as specific as possible. Who is in the room? Where are you? What time of day? What is the emotional sensation in your body?

2. What are positive replacements for smoking and drinking as a response to your physical, mental, or emotional cues?

3. Next to each new routine, list the rewards that accompany it. For example, instead of smoking, go for a walk. You'll be more fit, lose weight, and your overall health could improve.

25

EAT FOOD, NOT SUPPLEMENTS

- What vitamin supplements do you take?

- What foods supply sufficient vitamins and minerals in your diet?

It all comes back to what you eat,
what you drink, and what you think.

—Kris Carr

Americans invest more than 30 billion dollars a year on supplements—that could buy a whole lot of healthy food! If you walk down the vitamin aisle of your local grocery store or pharmacy, you'll see every supplement known to man and woman: magnesium, calcium, zinc, vitamins A, B, C, D, and E, and so many more! Buyer beware; they are only supplements. They are only good for closing dietary gaps. Nutrients from the actual source—food—should *always* be your first option.

Vitamins won't undo a poor diet

You never know who is eavesdropping in the doctor's office. I overheard a woman in the waiting room sharing her lunch plans to pick up fries and a burger. Interesting enough, it was same day she brought in a bag of vitamins to discuss—*literally, a whole bag*. She explained her reasons for adding each of them to her diet. I asked if she had ever considered a clean diet and jokingly mentioned her lunch plans. We chuckled at the obvious: her intention to use supplements as a substitute for healthier food choices. It's easier, right? Who doesn't want a shortcut? But taking vitamins won't undo a poor diet. I'm not disregarding the health benefits of vitamins. They have their place; I'll get to that later.

Eat real food

There is an element of truth in the adage "An apple a day keeps the doctor away." Fresh produce and whole foods contain fiber, vitamins, and minerals to support maximum health. But 67 percent of Americans are struggling with being overweight or obese, and most of our diets consist of high amounts of processed foods, refined grains, and sugars. These empty calories can potentially lead to a host of medical conditions. They also slow us down and cause inflammation. If you want to be your healthiest, don't take eating causally; pay attention—close attention—to what you eat.

Harmonize your diet

There are some things you simply can't get from a pill (or shouldn't). If you want your body to work better, the nutritional value of a balanced diet is unparalleled in trying to settle the score with supplements.

How do you achieve a healthy, harmonious blend with each meal? A picture-perfect nutritionally rich plate consists of one-quarter lean protein (baked or grilled meat, Greek yogurt, eggs, tofu) to build and repair; one-quarter whole-grain carbohydrates (pasta, barley, quinoa, couscous—sorry, cookies and ice cream aren't included) for energy; one-half fruits (some have more natural sugar than others, so select wisely) and vegetables for a healthy metabolism. Although it may not excite your taste buds, water should be your beverage of choice for hydration, calorie control, skin and muscle health, and kidney and bowel function. There's more to water than you can see and taste.

Enjoy every last bite or sip

There are easy and delicious ways to enjoy every last bite or sip of your nutrients instead of swallowing them in a capsule. (What is appetizing about that?) Pass on the chips and go for 70 percent dark chocolate or nuts. Have at least one green vegetable with every meal. Add spinach to your sandwich. Toss your favorite greens into a breakfast smoothie. Make your plate colorful, and eat veggies as close to their natural state as possible. The more they're cooked, the more nutrients will be in the broth. (Before you throw it out, use it for a soup or a smoothie!)

Occasionally treating yourself to a guilty pleasure is a very important part of balanced eating! A slice of red velvet cheesecake on my birthday is not the straw that'll break the camel's back—or send my nutrition completely out of whack. It is likely the one that will sustain my momentum.

When do supplements help?

I'll be the first to admit that a harmonized (well-balanced) diet doesn't always eliminate the need for vitamin supplements. As we gracefully mature, our appetite tends to decrease so that we eat less, which means we take in fewer nutrients. There are also health conditions that cause malabsorption, such as Crohn's and celiac disease, and food intolerances. Additionally, our dietary preferences, such as being vegetarian or vegan, can cause vitamin and mineral deficiencies. In these instances, supplements may or may not be the best solution. A nutritionist can help you sort it out.

Can you take too many vitamins?

Too much of a good thing can do more harm than good. You only want to ingest what *your* body is lacking. Toxic levels of vitamins in the blood can be very dangerous. On a similar note, some vitamins can interfere with prescribed medications. *I can't emphasize enough the importance of talking to your doctor before taking supplements.* Another word of caution: All vitamins are not created equal, so do your research.

Most of us can get exactly what we need through what we eat. Indulge in a variety of foods instead of looking for nutrition in a pill, because supplements are no substitute for healthy, harmonious eating.

"

The doctor of the
future will no longer
treat the human frame
with drugs,
but rather will
cure and prevent
disease with

nutrition.

—**Thomas Edison**

"

PRESCRIPTION

For Eat Food, Not Supplements

Most people aren't quite sure which vitamins and minerals can be found in foods, which foods may require a supplement, or how much of a particular nutrient is sufficient for a healthy, harmonized diet. It's too huge a topic to discuss at length in this book. I recommend looking up the Dietary Reference Intakes for information to guide you in the right direction. Keep in mind that not everyone needs or should take a supplement. Before signing up for a revolving monthly supply, increase your nutritional aptitude.

1. Why do you need a supplement in the first place? What's lacking? Stamina? A strong immune response? Healthy eating? Mental clarity?

2. Make a list of nutrients you believe are missing from your diet that could be causing the problem(s) you listed in question 1.

3. Are there foods you can eat to fill the nutritional deficit and correct the underlying concern? For example, if you want to increase your energy, a banana is a complex carb that contains vitamin B6 and potassium, which can give you an energy boost. The point? Before heading to the health food store, sniff out the pantry.

4. Plan your meals for the next five days. Even if you dine out or order takeout, you can still plan your meals.

5. Give some thought to how you have been feeling physically and mentally. In addition to planning what you'll eat, what food can you add to build your health? Sharpen your focus with fish; an ounce of almonds may help you sleep tight; oats could lift the blues.

Time to celebrate!

It's time to bring in some more positive reinforcement for being the incredible person you are right now. On this journey, be gracious toward yourself to avoid becoming physically and mentally exhausted. Affirm one of your wins—tiny or huge— by giving yourself a thumbs-up in the "Triumph" section.

SCIENCE SAYS...

"While supplement use contributes to an increased level of total nutrient intake, there are beneficial associations with nutrients from foods that aren't seen with supplements."

—Fan Chen, Fang Zhang, et al.
"Association Among Dietary Supplement Use, Nutrient Intake, and Mortality Among US Adults,"
Annals of Internal Medicine,
May 7, 2019, 170(9): 604–13

26

SPICE UP
YOUR LIFE

- What is your favorite spice?

- What are some spices with benefits—health benefits, that is?

> Fresh herbs really belong
> anywhere you put them.
> **—Alex Guarnaschelli**

Infuse your food with health and healing power! Herbs (plant leaves) and spices (roots, barks, seeds) make food taste better and you feel better. It's a burst of flavor with an antibacterial, antiviral, antioxidant, and anti-inflammatory twist. Herbs and spices also contain disease-fighting ingredients that fight against cancer and such chronic conditions as diabetes and heart disease. So don't just shake on the salt and pepper—the most common spices used in the United States with the least nutritional value. The right blend of seasonings can be chock-full of therapeutic benefits. A two for one: Eat a delicious meal and stay well at the same time.

Make your spice rack your pharmacy

A handful of chopped basil, a pinch of ginger, and a sprig of rosemary make for a tasty recipe for healthy living. Stock up and reach for your spice rack when you're looking for a boost. Which ones? Antioxidants in cinnamon have been linked to lowering inflammation as well as blood sugar in diabetics. Turmeric, the secret ingredient behind the golden hue of curry, is becoming more popular in American diets and, like cinnamon, curbs inflammation. Its medicinal profile also includes relieving colds, flu, and respiratory conditions and calming arthritis pain. And you can add ginger to your stash. It's commonly used in Caribbean cuisine, for good reason. It's delicious and is an excellent aide in settling an upset stomach. If ginger isn't your cup of tea, peppermint can also calm nausea and pain from inflammation.

Another global favorite is saffron, with roots in India. This spice is considered a mood booster and has been said to minimize symptoms of premenstrual syndrome (PMS) while also promoting learning and memory retention.

What are your thoughts on garlic? You may not mind having garlicky breath if it means lower cholesterol, lower blood pressure, and protection against heart disease. I'd say that's a good trade-off. If you're looking to steer clear of garlic (maybe because of a date?), consider spicy, sassy chili peppers and cumin. They can help you get your sexy back—or keep it—by pumping up your metabolism.

Greens aren't only garnish. Parsley inhibits cancer growth and strengthens immunity with its vitamins C, A, and K. Sage and rosemary are good to keep in the cabinet too. Sage may reduce bad cholesterol, and there's been scientific chatter that rosemary is associated with preserving brain health and easing stress—rosemary, take me away!

This is only a short list. Take note of your flavor favorites or a new spice you want to try, but don't go wild with spicing up your food just yet. Some herbs can interact with medications, so speak with your doctor before getting heavy-handed with nature's flavor profile.

Fresh + organic

The mouth-watering flavor of herbs and spices wakes up your palate and lessens the amount of salt, oils, and sweeteners required to savor food. Shop fresh and organic, but plan to use herbs and spices within a week. The longer they've sat on the shelves at the market or in your pantry, the more they'll lose some of their flavor and healing properties. Here's food for thought: Grow your own! I can't believe I suggested that since I'm minus two green thumbs, but maybe you have one. I hear gardening can be very therapeutic too. A double perk!

Pairing herbs and spices

You can do like I did: Raid the cupboard and toss in whatever spices you put your hands on first. But that doesn't usually work out well; trust me. I recommend a quick internet search to learn which herbs and spices pair well. For example, basil and mint; or garlic, parsley, and rosemary. It can save money, time, and perhaps even a headache caused by the wrong combo—if you do get a headache, cayenne, ginger, or peppermint oil may ease it.

No need to be a culinary genius

Even if you aren't a whiz in the kitchen—I'm certainly not— peppering your diet with herbs and spices can be fun. Sprinkle a little cinnamon, nutmeg, or clove in your morning coffee. Add mint leaves to a smoothie, cup of tea, or glass of water. Put some basil or rosemary on your sandwich. These simple options turn everyday foods into a delicious herbal feast that benefits your health.

Herbs are the friends
of the physician
and the pride of

cooks.

—**Charlemagne**

PRESCRIPTION

For Spicing Up Your Life

The fewer salt and salt-based seasonings you reach for, the better. Introduce one new spice or herb into your diet this week. Let it take center stage in your home-cooked foods, or ask the chef to toss a few into the dish. Play around with spices and herbs until you create something hearty and appetizing.

The following delicious herbs and spices are a great start to building your own spice bar (you'll recognize them from earlier in this chapter):

1. *Saffron*: A semisweet note, a pinch goes a very long way. This spice goes well with pasta dishes or hummus.

2. *Sage*: Pairs well with meats, roasted vegetables, and butternut squash; can be steeped in hot tea or water to soothe a sore throat.

3. *Rosemary*: A robust flavor that pulls out the best in most vegetables, meats, and pizza; one of my favorite fixings.

4. *Parsley:* A subtle multipurpose herb that complements just about any recipe, from quiche to marinades.

5. *Turmeric*: A healthy root that can be blended in smoothies, brewed in a tea, or sautéed in greens.

6. *Basil*: A tasty addition to soups, sandwiches, and salads.

7. *Vanilla bean*: There's no doubt you've seen this used multiple ways; pick one, or come up with your own creative ways to use this spice.

Next? Take one of your family recipes and add your own secret spice. Not only will it be the talk of the meal, but it'll put a healthy spin on the dish. Start with a hint of fresh herbs and spices, and add according to your taste buds. Do a little research to learn the best time to stir herbs and spices in to get the most zest.

27 SLEEP AND SEX ONLY

- What is your sleep regimen?

- Besides sleep and sex, what activities take place in your bedroom?

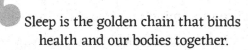

Sleep is the golden chain that binds
health and our bodies together.

—T. Dekker

"Sleep is overrated," says the person who keeps hitting the snooze button. Wake-up call! It's that lack of respect for sleep that keeps us from functioning and living at our true potential. Life is too short, and there's too much to do to be sleep deprived and not enjoy every blissful wakening moment. Even as child, I appreciated falling into the magical restfulness of sleep, and its refreshing ability has continued to earn my awe. Some may say I'm a few winks shy of being a sleepaholic, but I think of myself as a sleep *enthusiast*—a connoisseur of that delicate sweet spot between not enough and too much sleep.

Sleep is your oyster

Sleep is often the sacrificial offering. Burning the midnight oil has long been held in high regard. But rest assured, the well-rested should not lose admiration. Getting sufficient shut-eye is not being lazy or a waste of time. It's the throttle for creativity and productivity. Eventually, skating by on less than 40 winks (a full night's sleep) is a surefire way to crash and burn.

Sleep is your oyster. You need the right amount of it to do what you want to do, go where you want to go, and stay healthy while doing so. Depriving yourself of sleep can take a serious toll on the mind and body. I'm not speaking of bags or dark circles under your eyes but of more significant health consequences, such as forgetfulness, delayed reactions, depression, diabetes, obesity, and heart problems. Without ample sleep, you can find yourself in poor health and asleep at the wheel life.

If you don't snooze, you lose

Seven to nine hours of nightly siesta is as necessary as air and food. The daily hustle—work, the kids' after-school activities, errands—exhausts our bodies and stretches us thin (figuratively speaking). Good sleep hygiene replenishes, repairs, and recharges. Catching enough Zs can pay it forward in ways that might surprise you: a better sex life (should I stop there?), improved mood, clearer thinking, increased performance, and fewer injuries. Good things happen with enough sleep.

Sex and sleep only

It's time for the "talk." All kinds of shenanigans occur in the bedroom that disrupt sleep, from working on your laptop while in bed or scrolling on social media to binge-watching movies. If it is not sleep or sex, kick it out of the bedroom. No exceptions. Your brain and body should naturally relax and prepare for either romance or dreamland by walking toward the boudoir because they are conditioned to expect those as the only two options.

If we throw our brains a lot of curve balls by having the bedroom serve too many purposes, it can be caught off guard when it's actually time to sleep. I was skimming a blog by Jerome Doraisamy in *The Wellness Doctrines* when I read an interesting concept: ". . . we need to ensure physical (and therefore emotional) separation between the daily grind and our downtime. Overlap between the two increases the chance we will not be able to tell when we can kickback which, in my experience, has made falling asleep much harder at times." In other words, our environment plays a role in signaling to our brains what to turn on and what to shut down.

Establish (and stick to) a sleep schedule

Sticking to a routine will help you avoid getting caught between the sheets counting sheep, which is neither healthy nor fun. One way to stop thrashing about in bed is to rise and shine as well as hit the hay at the same time every day (or night), including the weekends. It keeps your brain's 24-hour internal clock—circadian rhythm—in a synchronized cycle between alertness and sleepiness. Take your sleep even deeper, and consider the support and comfort of your mattress. A bad mattress can cause tossing and turning as well as body and joint pain—no one wants to wake up feeling like they've been in a fight.

Create a sleep sanctuary

Make your personal sanctuary sleep-friendly by setting the mood as dark, quiet, and cool. When you drift off to sleep, your body temperature drops, and if the heat is turned down five to ten degrees, you'll doze off sooner. In the same vein, skip the hot shower right before bed. It raises the body temperature; instead, shower an hour before bedtime. And unless you've fumbled with your wiring, the body is conditioned to snooze in a dark, quiet room, so cut off the lights, lower the noise, and sleep tight.

There are additional tips for creating the right ambience. I have added a few extra touches to my sleep haven: a diffuser (a hint of lavender), a soft rug for meditation, and a sound machine (there's nothing more calming to me than the sound of the ocean). I am also considering repainting the wall to a more soothing color; perhaps, a soft flat blue. I heard from other sleep enthusiasts that people who slumber in rooms painted blue sleep the longest—that's reason enough for me to change the paint color.

Three meals
plus bedtime
make for
4 sure blessings
each

day.

—**Mason Cooley**

PRESCRIPTION

For Sleep and Sex Only

Let's turn all this talk into action by creating a perfect sleep cocoon. Before diving into tasks, close your eyes and visualize what your cozy bedroom will look like. Once you have a vision . . .

1. Choose a date to ditch the television and electronics from the bedroom. If you sense resistance from your spouse, reassure them that this is a small trade-off for the potential of more sex and less crankiness.

2. What are some ways you can create a serene bedroom: Use soft and warm (shades of blue or green), flat (not glossy) paint; build the best bedding that breathes well and wicks moisture; add scented candles, fresh flowers, or beautiful wall decor?

3. How can you block light from entering the room, including the light from your clock, watch, and digital screens (perhaps leave them in another room)?

4. Find that comfy temperature between 60 and 67 degrees Fahrenheit (not too cold, not too hot). If you don't want to hear others in the house complaining about being cold, open your bedroom window or turn on the ceiling fan.

5. Filter out as much background noise as possible. Put the phone on silent and turn off alerts.

6. Is your mattress more than ten years old? Pillows flat? Stop flipping and fluffing; get new ones or try a mattress topper.

Now that you know how to make your bedroom more restful, stop staring at the ceiling. Go to sleep, have sex, or get out of the bedroom!

SCIENCE SAYS...

"Eighty percent of all Americans
said they have sleep problems
at least once a week."

—2018 nationally represented *Consumer Reports* survey
of 1,767 US adults

28

LOVE THE SKIN
YOU LIVE IN

- What is your skincare regimen?

- How has your skincare routine evolved with aging?

Healthy skin is a reflection
of overall wellness.

—Howard Murad, MD

Raise your glass to aging like a fine wine! Wouldn't it be incredible to find the perfect anti-aging elixir? Take it from me, a doctor who has layered on product after product (I'm a bit of a skincare addict) in pursuit of the *glow factor*. Supple, youthful skin cannot be manufactured entirely from an arsenal of creams, lotions, and serums. The natural, healthy radiance you are trying to purchase starts with treating your skin to the lifestyle and care it deserves. Your skin is not simply a sheath to cover the body; it's actually your largest organ—you need to treat it that way!

My mentor, Dr. Howard Murad (founder of Murad Skincare and Father of Modern Wellness), said it best, "You must think of skincare as health care. What damages your skin ultimately penetrates into the bloodstream and damages every organ in your body. By the same token, when any organ is damaged, it will show up on the skin." Your skin is a tattletale—listen.

Seven steps to skin heaven
From the foods you eat, to keeping a lid on stress, to your daily skincare potions, you either reverse the signs of aging or speed them up. A dollop of healthy, harmonious living can bring out that rosy complexion you so admire. Between you and me, I have some health and wellness secrets that can erase years—everybody could use one or two magicked away—off your skin. And these tips come straight from the guru himself, Dr. Murad!

Here are the Seven Steps to Skin Heaven:

1. *Hydrate, hydrate, hydrate.* The best water for your skin isn't necessarily in a bottle or from the tap. According to Dr. Murad, you should both "drink and eat your water."
   - Did you know watermelon and cucumbers are 97 percent water and tomatoes and zucchini are 95 percent water? Water can be tasty!
   - Fruit and vegetables are an excellent source of water that will replenish the cells and make their membranes stronger.

Keeping the body hydrated also prevents cells from deteriorating and producing wrinkles—need I say more!

2. *Eat a diet tailored for healthy skin.* Oranges, pomegranates, goji berries, and apricots are packed with vitamin C and other antioxidants that defend against cell oxidation and sun damage. Since the body cannot produce antioxidants, it is important to eat them. With each mouthful, your skin will begin to look and feel younger!

3. *Exercise for gorgeous skin.* Exercise improves blood circulation, thereby increasing the delivery of nutrients to the skin and removing debris. Exercise is like oxygen for the skin. It allows the cells to release energy for a more luminous appearance.

4. *Hibernate like a bear, nightly.* Remember the "Sleep and Sex Only" chapter? Beauty sleep is a real thing. Seven to nine hours of sleep reverses free-radical damage, builds new cells, and repairs connective tissue.

5. *De-stress your look.* Dr. Murad coined the phrase "cultural stress" to define the constant and pervasive stress of being connected to obligations 24 hours a day, 7 days a week. Stress weakens the cells and makes it difficult for the body to repair and rejuvenate. Streamlining your schedule is a step in the direction of lustrous skin. Now would also be a good time to meditate.

6. *Keep your skin under cover.* Wear a sunblock. There are moisturizers and foundations that have them built in. While sunlight triggers the body's production of vitamin D and elicits a lovely skin color, it also causes age spots, sagging, and skin cancer, which can be irreversible. Wear sun protection *daily* of at least 30 SPF, and *reapply* it after two hours. I skipped this step while in a Hawaii and got my first sunburn.

7. *Take your skincare regimen personally.* No one face cream fits all. Determine your skin type, and target your skin concerns. Further, your skincare routine should change with seasons, illness, and age. As life transitions, so should your skincare regimen.

Smoking and alcohol damage skin

It should go without saying (but I will say it anyway), smoking or excessive use of alcohol isn't pretty. They ruin your looks by starving your skin of nutrients and oxygen. The next time you light up or toss a few back, remember: *Not only is it unhealthy, it accelerates signs of aging.*

The products you put on your skin are as important as how you care for your body. When skincare becomes synonymous with health care, clear and youthful skin is your reward!

Botox and fillers

I wasn't going to mention Botox and fillers, but I know wrinkles and folds can send us over the edge. Everyone from the dentist to the hairstylist has an opinion about your beauty, but there are a few things you should know before imbibing from the fountain of Botox and dermal fillers.

In the name of transparency, I am not a regular, but I have used them. As a doctor, I know it's important to choose a reputable person to apply such treatments; otherwise, things can go south quickly. Ask if the person is an official vendor. You want to make sure you are getting the right product. To prevent bruising, know what medicine, food, and drinks to avoid prior to the procedure. Don't overdo it. Used wisely, Botox and fillers can refresh your appearance. Think of them as tools to soften your look, not wands to reconstruct it.

Aging is a
fact of life.
Looking your
age is

not.

—Howard Murad, MD

PRESCRIPTION

For Loving the Skin You Live In

The best combination to unlock beautiful skin is Dr. Murad's 2-2-2-1-7 code: Cleanse *twice* daily, apply products to address your skin needs *twice* daily, use hydration/protection treatments *twice* daily, exfoliate *once* weekly, and every *seven* weeks pamper your skin with a professional facial.

When you take care of the skin you live in, you will not only look healthier but will also feel better. To put your best face forward, jot down this basic skincare plan in your journal:

1. Identify your skin type: normal, dry, oily, or combination. Talk with your dermatologist or aesthetician about the best treatment for your skin.

2. Take note of products, foods, or environmental exposures that offend your skin. Things that once were not damaging could become harmful.

3. Change your pillowcases weekly, pull your hair away from your face while sleeping, and avoid sleeping face-down (anything to stave off wrinkles).

4. Look at the whole picture when evaluating your skin—both the internal and external factors.

5. Discuss unfavorable changes with your physician and options to minimize or eliminate them.

6. In your 20s, give your skin plenty of UVA and UVB protection. In your 30s, add anti-aging products (vitamin C and green tea). In your 40s, go heavy on collagen-building ingredients (peptides and retinol). In your 50s, lather on the hydration (niacinamide and hyaluronic acid). When you're 60+, continue to volumize and moisturize the face (retinoids and rose oil).

We must get older—although I've been holding at 30 for years—but we can do so gracefully!

29

MENTAL
MAINTENANCE

- Do you have scheduled maintenance for your mental well-being?

- How do you maintain mental harmony?

> Learn to calm down the winds
> of your mind, and you
> will enjoy great inner peace.
>
> —**Remez Sasson**

Positive vibes, positive rays, and positive mood—that *is* what's printed on the T-shirt. But a T-shirt doesn't make it so. Living life with a sense of contentment and mental blissfulness is more than wearing a slogan. You probably would have preferred to have known that before you purchased a T-shirt in every color. No need to return them, because this Prescription is intended to show you how to wear them with pride.

We take our cars to the shop for a tune-up, service our homes, update our phones, and most of us even schedule a yearly health checkup. Yet our mental well-being is left to its own devices. It's not healthy for the long haul.

When you just keep going and going like the Energizer Bunny, you eventually hit a brick wall called "burnout"—emotionally drained, mentally exhausted (and physically fatigued). Mental harmony isn't a bottomless wellspring. It requires maintenance.

Time for mental upkeep

How do you know when it's time for some mental upkeep? Thank goodness there are clues; however, you don't have to wait for a sign to retreat to your quiet little corner of the world. But if you need one, take your pick of these: dreading to get out of bed, feeling like you have nothing else to give, wishing the day was over before it starts, an overall pessimistic attitude, small tasks seeming big, drastic behaviors, forgetfulness, and an inner void. By all means, this isn't a complete list, but hopefully it's a hint of what to look for. My advice is try not to let it come to this. Recovery is no walk in the park.

Collect your thoughts

There is so much competing for your mental sanity. News headlines, social media feeds, deadlines, real life, and responsibilities. Life mounts up, and it's easy for the mind to become flooded. There's barely a moment to collect your thoughts, and you become mentally out of shape just trying to keep up the pace. Regular mental maintenance softens the mental blows from stress. It's your buffer from everything that's going on in your world.

Mental stamina

I remember a story about a woman stranded in a Hawaiian forest for 17 days—a nice place to visit, but a not-so-cool place to be deserted. She survived on plants, berries, and water. It's not so farfetched to think that many of us, in the same situation, might have called it quits, but she had an ace up her sleeve. Likely unbeknownst to herself, her secret weapon was meditation. Doesn't sound like a bad idea now to have the "Meditate Day and Night" Prescription in your wellness toolkit. She used meditation to strengthen her mind in order to pull through a difficult dilemma. Our inner resources can stimulate mental push-ups that keep the mind operating smoothly even in the toughest situations. Building mental stamina isn't only good when you're in trouble; it's also good for managing the daily shuffle that sometimes makes you want to scream—if you need to, scream.

Your most prized possession

A well mind is one of your—and my—most prized possession. I don't know about you, but taking care of my mental health is one of the first things out the window when I'm in a crunch. After my mother broke her hip, I traveled eight hours, round-trip, nearly every weekend for months to be there for her—she's always been there for me. I had little time for anything, never mind mental maintenance. Oh boy, what a mistake! On one of the drives back home, I found myself on the side of the highway in tears—mentally bankrupt, not an iota of anything left for me. It was a lesson well learned: Mental maintenance isn't optional, and making it so is a threat to your mental health.

What does mental maintenance look like?

Now that you know it isn't a given and it is best to schedule it, what does everyday mental maintenance look like? While it's important to note that it looks and feels different for everyone and it changes according to your needs, there are some solid guidelines. Whether your mental maintenance is sitting and reflecting, dancing around the room, or a morning stretch, the only rule is that whatever you choose recharges you and releases emotional build-up. It should also be easy to incorporate into your daily routine—not mentally taxing.

Temporarily closing for mental maintenance adjusts your sails to remain fluid and seize the moments.

Yesterday is
heavy.
Put it

down.

—**Clarence Fell**

PRESCRIPTION

For Mental Maintenance

A plan makes it official. You've moved from talking to action. You have some ideas in mind and a strategy to achieve it. So what's your daily mental maintenance plan? Don't have one? Not to worry; let's put one together right now.

1. What are 10 to 20 things that bring you mental serenity (practical things that can be done daily and within 15 to 30 minutes)?

2. Get out your phone or wherever you keep your calendar. I still prefer pen and paper. Seeing things in my own handwriting makes them feel a bit more personal.

3. For each day of the week, write down an activity from the list you created in question 1.

4. Be specific about the way you will include each activity into your day. When? Where? How?

5. After you have finished the mental maintenance activity, in one word sum up how you felt; put it on your calendar next to the activity.
6. Repeat this at the end of each week.
7. Continue to grow your list of things that lift your mood.

Stick to your plan to embrace life as it comes.

Time to celebrate!

This is a good opportunity to take a break and use some enlightenment from this Prescription for a mental tune-up. You've traveled quite a distance on your personal journey.

It has been said that seeing is believing, go to the "Triumphs" page to write down the strides you're making. Cap it off with a fun private—or public—celebration! Flowers? A cupcake? A night of dancing? Whatever feels most appropriate to you.

SCIENCE SAYS...

"Ninety-three percent of the most resilient Americans believe mental health is as important as physical health."

—"State of Health: Resilience" special report, *Everyday Health* and Ohio State University, 2019

30

TRAUMATIZED
BY TRAUMA

- What did the trauma take from you?

- How do you get closure from trauma?

> There are wounds that never
> show on the body that are deeper
> and more hurtful than anything
> that bleeds.
>
> **—Laurell K. Hamilton**

Life isn't a bowl of cherries (no surprise). Bad things will knock at your door—whether or not you answer, unpleasant events will find a way in. They will shake your sense of security, call into question how you see people and the world, and make you wonder how something so devastating is even possible. Life isn't all sunshine, but sometimes rainstorms produce the brightest rainbows.

Nothing is wrong with you

Plain and simple . . . tragedy will strike. Trauma is *anything* that threatens your emotional, physical, or psychological harmony. While there are traumatic events (sexual assault, racial injustices) that would be a struggle for anyone to shake off, all trauma isn't universal—what's traumatic for one person is not necessarily another person's experience. Sensitivity to the different faces of trauma sidesteps judging, comparing, and re-traumatizing. Nothing is wrong with you. Your hurt and pain are allowed. Your trauma is valid; you don't have to just suck it up—and you shouldn't.

Triggers

"Let sleeping dogs lie." Because if they're awakened, you could relive the trauma all over again. Whenever I encounter rejection, it dredges up memories of what it felt like to be a fatherless daughter—that's how the neglect felt to me. And although the intensity of my emotions has quieted and the wound is no longer fresh, there are aftershocks—mini earthquakes that follow big ones. Even when the actual trauma has ceased, there are triggers that, if activated, can pull the trigger again.

When you experience a reaction, it isn't out of the blue. Becoming familiar with, understanding, and creating a plan of action will give your triggers less and less power over you. You can disarm the smell, the sarcasm, the humiliation, the tone—the trigger. It's a sign of post-traumatic growth, a positive transformation after a collision with life.

You minus the trauma

After having stared down trauma in its cold, dark eyes, a connection is established between you and that trauma—you co-exist. There is no you minus the trauma. Your life is forever changed, and your innocence won't be returned. The time before the physical and sexual abuse, the neglect, the rejection, the betrayal, the assault, the injustices—the sheer hell—is nevermore. And as badly as you may wish it hadn't happened to you, it did. Your only option is to make those parts of your life that were attacked better.

It wasn't your fault

Fear. Shame. Guilt. It wasn't your fault. You are not in any way to blame for someone abusing your trust, hurting you, or both. I knew someone would need to read that—if it is you, read it again. If you have been holding yourself responsible, I want you to take this moment to breathe and start to free yourself of the blame. No, there is absolutely nothing you should have done differently. Refuse to be convinced otherwise.

Happiness after trauma

It may be hard to imagine, but there is happiness after trauma. Your life is not over by a long shot—it is not the end of you. And after going through something so difficult, you owe it to yourself to heal and reconnect to joy. *You're still standing.* Take a moment to appreciate that. The crisis may have temporarily taken you down, but it didn't take you out of the game entirely. With the fight that's left in you—and yes, there is still some left—you get to choose the ending to your story!

Trauma creates
a rupture in
a person's life

story.

—**Stephen Joseph**

PRESCRIPTION

For Traumatized by Trauma

Let's begin putting the pieces of your life back together. The goal is not to get you back to where you were before the trauma but to guide you to a place where you feel safe enough to let go of the tragic situation so you can rebuild your life. Breathe. Take it slow. And move forward.

Do not push yourself too hard to complete this Prescription. Yes, it's important to complete it, but it's also important to be kind to yourself. This Prescription is here when you are ready. Depending on your situation, it may be best for you to speak with a therapist.

What was the trauma? Describe it in as little or as much detail as you feel comfortable providing.

How did the trauma change your personality?

When the trauma occurred, I felt_____.
List five emotions.

It is challenging to co-exist with the crisis because...

What did the trauma take from you?

What triggers your trauma?

Who do you need to forgive in order to recover from the trauma?

As a result of the trauma, what scares you most now?

31

HEALTHY RELATIONSHIPS

ARE GOOD FOR THE BODY AND SOUL

- Who were your closest childhood friends?

- How often do you connect with friends off-line?

It's the friends you can call up
at 4 a.m. that matter.

—Marlene Dietrich

Meeting up with two dear friends and baring your heart can be better than taking two aspirin and calling your doctor in the morning. Talking with trusted friends can do wonders for the body and soul. But how often do we stop and evaluate our friendships to ensure they pass the "healthy" test? Very rarely, if at all.

Is your social circle loving and supportive? Can you count on your inner network for better or for worse? Are you in relationships with people who belittle or don't even consider your feelings? You deserve to answer these questions, because you deserve to know if you're in a lopsided relationship—one that's only benefiting the other person. That's not healthy.

I understand that no friendship is perfect, but a healthy one should feel enjoyable to both people *most* of the time. In large part because you accept each other for who you are, imperfections and all, and do not pressure each other to be who you expect them to be.

Life is better with friends

There is something very special about knowing there is someone in this world who has your back. My best friend from childhood, Gloria Jean, definitely had mine until her passing. When we met, I couldn't have imagined that a childhood friendship would weather so many seasons without us losing track of each other. There were times when we weren't in contact, but it didn't mean our connection was lost. She was always by my side, encouraging me to spread my wings. I hope she knew the tremendous strength I drew from our relationship.

I miss Gloria Jean, but I still feel her spirit living life with me—that's true friendship.

Having an entourage—not necessarily large, just loyal—in your corner who loves, values, respects, supports, and has your best interests at heart is favorable for living longer, healthier, and happier. Your tribe isn't just along for the ride; when the stakes are high, healthy friendships carry the moment.

Think of friendships as the colorful sprinkles on your cupcake. They make life more beautiful, fun, and sweet. They are also your ember of light in dark moments. Life is so much better with close friends and can feel impossible without them.

Be true to yourself

Are you a good friend to yourself? The relationship you have with yourself will be the gold standard to judge your relationships with others. When you lose touch with yourself, it's difficult to have meaningful ties with other people. That's why working on being a rock-solid friend to yourself is all-important. It sets the bar for the company you keep and the quality of the bonds you form. Having said that, unhealthy dynamics in relationships usually stem from the way people feel about themselves.

Where do you begin?

As I previously mentioned, start with being your own bestie. When you have that under your belt (and believe me, it's not as easy as you might think), then make expanding your circle a priority. If you desire relationships that'll pay dividends for the rest of your life (who doesn't?), they will require regular care and maintenance, but you'll get out of it what you are willing to put into it. If you're lucky, you each will get far more than either expected.

I'm fond of the parallel Maud Purcell draws between growing healthy friendships and nurturing gardens: "Find fertile soil. Add sunlight. Plant seeds. Fertilize. Water. Weed." Friends should have common interests, brighten your spirit, be dependable (during the ups and downs), be handled with care, be celebrated, and have mutual respect despite differences. When that happens, you'll have a lovely bloom to enjoy!

A health investment

No, you cannot do it alone, and it's not recommended that you try to go through life without friendship. Camaraderie is as equally important as a healthy diet, regular exercise, and adequate sleep. In fact, evidence shows that lack of a strong social cohort can be as detrimental to your health as smoking. Healthy relationships help to calm anxiety and depression, manage stress, improve sleep, boost the immune system, lower risk of dementia, and can even add years to your life. Now that's a friendship worth having!

It's good for your health to have friends you can trust with your dreams and your struggles, people who depend on you—and on whom you can depend—who understand, challenge, and appreciate you and who know just what to say and when to say it.

Companionships like those make a world of difference. I called that type of friend Jenean—she's my bestie, and she gets me even when I don't get myself.

Friendship with benefits

Worthwhile relationships are rarely fortuitous; they require an investment of your time. To have a friendship with benefits (healthy benefits, that is), schedule a standing engagement to stay connected with your bestie, your amigo, your ride-or-die. While you're at it, make sure to include some real face time. Because whatever else you are busy doing, it's not as important to your health as carving out time to spend with a friend! I love Sunday evening talks with Kim, check-ins with Penny, photos and conversations with Stephanie, and skincare shopping with Michele—wouldn't trade this time for the world.

A friend is a person
with whom I
may be sincere.
Before him,
I may think

aloud.

— **Ralph Waldo Emerson**

PRESCRIPTION

For Having Healthy Relationships

A healthy relationship may be just what the doctor ordered—it's definitely what *this* doctor prescribes! A heaping dose of friendship, repeated as often as you like, is both heartwarming and healthful. Your friends are your biggest asset! So get back in touch with your favorite people.

1. Make a list of your closest friends (not necessarily the ones you are in contact with the most). Limit your list to no more than 10 people. It doesn't matter who's written first or last; this is not a scale of importance.

2. Now, go through your list and assign a "health grade" to each person.

   A. The friendship is in peak shape. There's a true soul-to-soul connection.

B. The friendship could use a pick-me-up. It's time to catch up.

C. The friendship needs some real face time. Things are starting to feel awkward.

D. The friendship is barely hanging on. You've hardly been in contact except through social media.

3. How can you rekindle the friendships with a health grade of B, C, or D?

4. Put yourself out there. Send a text or give them a call to let them know you miss them and would like to reconnect.

5. When the relationship is back up and healthier, keep it afloat by planning regular outings (for example, coffee, lunches, or weekend getaways) or phone conversations (FaceTime too). Do not cancel unless it is absolutely necessary.

SCIENCE SAYS...

"Lacking social connection carries a risk that is comparable, and in many cases, exceeds that of other well-accepted risk factors, including smoking up to 15 cigarettes per day, physical inactivity, and air pollution."

—J. Holt-Lunstad, T. B. Smith, and J. B. Layton [2010]. "Social relationships and mortality risk: a meta-analytic review", *PLoS Medicine*, 7(7). e1000316. doi: 10.1371/journalmed. 1000316

32

UNTIL WE MEET AGAIN

- How is grief supposed to feel?

- When will the grieving end?

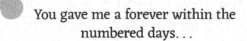

You gave me a forever within the numbered days. . .

—John Green,
The Fault in Our Stars

It is impossible to fully express how dearly we behold the love, joy, and loyalty of our loved ones and friends. What a blessing to share our lives with such special people! And even though we know that death is a part of the circle of life, when they are no longer physically present with us, the void can feel eternal, and our hearts are left to search for comfort.

Woefully, we will all hear the words, "I'm sorry for your loss." As an adult, when I first heard these condolences, I was unsure of how to receive them. They didn't make me feel any better. It seemed unfair that somehow I was to push through my tremendous losses and heal when I didn't want to say goodbye but had to. But I am grateful that there's joy after mourning.

I'm not fine yet

How are *you*? I'm not fine yet. Grieving takes time, and no one can tell you how much. The grief journey is a personal one, and you can't rush it. This doesn't mean you have go through it alone, and you shouldn't, but support is different for each person. It has nothing to do with how well you're handling your loss. People may be quick to judge—largely because they are uncomfortable with seeing someone in pain. You may hear things like "You should be better by now." "You need to get back to living your life." "It is unhealthy to still be grieving this intensely." If those phrases come up, don't feel pressured to move on. There is no specific timetable for grieving.

Grieving is healthy

"Sympathy is a little medicine to soothe the ache in another's heart." Over and over again, I've had to reassure patients that grieving is one of the healthiest things they can do when they have suffered a significant loss. Life has taken a turn—expectedly or unexpectedly—and sorrow is normal. It's human. And if you believe that there is a reason for everything, then grieving also serves a purpose. It is therapeutic and a part of the transition into your forever-changed world.

Ask for help

A meeting of the heart and mind can be difficult to obtain, especially when loss is involved, and the imbalance can leave an opening for grief to descend into depression. If you're paralyzed by the chronic presence of sorrow (cannot get out of bed, can't go to work, can't eat enough to avoid serious weight loss, or have thoughts of taking your life), it's possible your grief has taken a turn for the worse. There is no shame in asking for help and seeking professional guidance.

Survivor's guilt

Grief alone is stressful. Grief plus guilt is a tormenting sadness that weighs so heavily on your heart that your heartbeat feels almost too faint to sustain life.

As I write this book, the world is in the midst of the global COVID-19 pandemic. Hundreds of thousands of families are grieving the loss of loved ones due to a virus that seemingly has no rhyme or reason for its fatalities. Many are left to recover while carrying the burden of survivor's guilt. Some didn't have an opportunity to be at their family member's bedside or have a proper funeral due to the fear of risking more lives, and that sorrow—which lacks closure—can feel unbearable. To then have to quarantine with guilt-ridden feelings is nothing less than merciless. The world will bear the scars of COVID-19 for a long time, because surviving any tragedy that claims so many lives is a complicated grieving process.

Expunging self-guilt and finding peace after any tragic event is hard, but you wouldn't want a loved one to blame themselves for something that was not their fault. You shouldn't, either.

Grieving when no one died

It was on a Mother's Day when my world turned upside down. My heart paused. I felt lifeless. Because in that moment I somehow knew, beyond a shadow of a doubt, that being a biological mother wasn't in the cards for me. I cannot explain it.

There was no upsetting news from my doctor. I wasn't even trying to become pregnant. Nothing out of the ordinary had happened, other than I was moving beyond childbearing age. But on that Mother's Day, I experienced the painstaking loss of Kennedy or Lily—the names I'd chosen for my baby girl, which I knew I would no longer need. I still turn around when I hear them.

I understand that there is more than one way to be a mother, but I wasn't ready to consider those yet, and it took me years to accept the other options. Notably, acceptance is the last stage of grief. Today I'm grateful for the grace to accept an alternative version of my life and accept my un-accidental reality. Perhaps now is a good time for you (and me, too) to look again at the "Accept What You Cannot Change" Prescription.

The point is that losses come in many shapes and forms, and the absence of a funeral service doesn't make them any less real or lessen the magnitude of your pain. For me, grieving when nobody had died felt more isolating and heart-wrenching.

G.R.I.E.F. kit
There are ways to make coping with your loss a little easier on the heart.

- *G— Give* yourself time to adapt to the loss. Don't try to rush it; doing so can make you feel worse. Your heart won't heal overnight, but it will heal.
- *R— Recognize* how things will be different. It can be scary to do things for the first time or to do them alone. Take baby steps.
- *I — Involve* yourself in activities that you've been putting off, or resume some that you enjoyed.
- *E— Express* your loss in healthy ways, such as journaling, being more physically active, and, yes, crying.
- *F — Find* a support group. Talking with people who have been through something similar and survived can give you a shoulder to lean on.

A tip for when your friend is grieving

Be supportive without telling your friend *how* to grieve. It is a process that is unique to each person. And when you need it, there will be someone to do the same for you.

How lucky I am
to have something
that makes
saying goodbye so

hard.

—**Winnie the Pooh**

PRESCRIPTION

For Until We Meet Again

It may seem like you'll never laugh, take a deep breath, or fully live again, but the pain of sorrow does subside, and joy and peace will take its place. In the meantime, it is best not to try to bury what are you feeling inside your heart. Here are some steps to navigate your grief:

Write down the loss you are grieving or what happened that you have not allowed yourself to grieve.

What will you miss the most?

How will your life be different?

What are you most afraid of?

When you're ready—and not a moment before—write a goodbye letter. Share feelings, memories, things left unsaid; include
how you will honor their life or the lesson you learned.

33

I'M NOT
SAD

- Do people tell you that you seem sad?

- What is your depression a response to?

The only thing more exhausting
than being depressed
is pretending that you're not.

—Anonymous

When I ask about the "D" word, the apparent changes in my patients' body languages and facial expressions show their internal struggle with how to respond. If I say "yes," does it mean I am a weak person, or, heaven forbid, does a "yes" mean I am crazy? If I say "no," will these feelings of helplessness, hopelessness, and worthlessness fence me in forever? Depression bears no relation to being weak or strong. Depression has no connection to being crazy—whatever that means. Depression usually won't go away without help. Depression is nothing to be ashamed of.

Sometimes you're simply in a sad mood and a good cry will do. But other times, being unhappy isn't just the blues; it is a sign of something more—a sign of depression. It shouldn't be taken lightly or come to a big mess before it's taken seriously; like high blood pressure and diabetes, depression is an illness. Your mind is deserving of the same care that presumedly you would give your body.

Don't let the stigma keep you depressed
So that we are clear, sadness and depression are not synonymous; it's important to differentiate the two. The mindless reflex to downplay your depression to sadness is understandable. Societal stigma around mental health is anything but kind and gentle. It's insensitive. But that's their problem, not yours.

Millions, yes millions, of people suffer from depression. If you're one of them, obviously you're not alone. But sadly, it is frequently swept under the rug and goes untreated until it trips you up and sucks the life right out of you. If you want a fighting chance at finding your healthy place, don't let the stigma keep you depressed. Don't let it keep you from getting help.

Eight signs your sadness is depression

If you cannot shake these symptoms after two weeks, it's time to do something about your mood.

1. *Sleeping too little or too much.* Changes in sleep pattern can clue you in on depression. Ask yourself if you're using sleep to escape from problems? Or are you too troubled to fall asleep? Both lanes lead to depression. Also notice whether your sleep feels refreshing. Is it disrupted by awakening multiple times, causing you to be fatigued and irritable?

2. *Lack of interest in activities that were pleasurable.* If you'd rather not hang out with friends or participate in your favorite pastimes or hobbies, it could be a red flag that you're not just down in the dumps but depressed.

3. *A guilty conscious.* Do you constantly feel guilty about things, even when they are not in your control? Being consumed by a guilty conscious is a signal that depression may be lurking. People with depression tend to get stuck in a cycle of excessive negative thoughts that weigh heavily on their mind and distort their thinking.

4. *Low energy.* If the low-battery light seems to always be on in your life, check to make certain you aren't depressed— not feeling motivated can be a tell-tale sign. The thought process is typically slower in depressed persons, making it difficult to get simple day-to-day tasks done.

5. *Poor concentration.* Are you staring at the same thing for hours and can't make headway? This could possibly be a warning sign—depression ahead. When you are easily distracted, the ability to comprehend and retain information is affected. Poor concentration can put a burden on work, personal life, and relationships, leaving you feeling alienated.

6. *Overeating or loss of appetite.* Food is a common way to numb emotions. If your eating is largely unrelated to hunger but instead you crave its comfort, you may very well be depressed. Likewise, if you are dropping weight due to a lack of appetite, a cloud of depression may be hanging over you.

7. *Easily agitated.* When the "normal chaos" is frustrating you more than usual and you frequently feel seconds from crying, it might be a sign that you're depressed. The fatigue, perceived stress, and persistently low mood—hallmarks of depression—can be keeping you on edge.

8. *Suicidal thoughts.* Take thoughts of hurting yourself very seriously. Do not try to decipher whether or not you are depressed. Seek professional help immediately. With the appropriate intervention, you can regain hope and self-worth.

Climb out of bed and get back on track

You cannot fix your life without facing up to where healing is needed. You'll climb out of bed and get back on track much sooner when you grasp that you're not just sad, you're depressed. Then you can make the most of each mustard seed of energy—small efforts can grow into big progress—that you have to restore a sound and clear mind.

Schedule an appointment with your health provider to discuss treatment options and therapy. Increase your physical activity to boost your mood (you don't have to run a marathon, just get your blood circulating). Stick to a daily routine—it'll help you focus. Connect with friends and family so you aren't isolated. Get out of the pajama bottoms and T-shirt; spruce yourself up. Eat healthily, especially foods high in folic acid (spinach and broccoli) and omega-3 fatty acids (salmon and walnuts), and avoid drugs and alcohol.

Depression doesn't have to keep you down for the count. You can live to fight another day, a happier one.

When people
don't know exactly
what depression is,
they can be

judgmental.

—**Marion Cotillard**

PRESCRIPTION

33

For I'm Not Sad

Now is a good time for a journal moment. Hopefully you already have it out; if not, pull it out and let's win back your knack for enjoying life. Kick it into gear with this M.O.O.D. Q&A.

- *M: Monitor* your mood and how long you have been feeling down. Are you sad, disappointed, hopeless, depressed? Not sure if those words fit, put it in your own words. Have you been in this mood for more than two weeks?

- *O: Observe* and write down your thoughts and feelings (minus the sugarcoating). Where are your emotions stemming from? What are you overdoing (eating, sleeping, isolating, alcohol, sex, shopping) to cope with being in a dark place. How do you react to a real downer in your life?

- *O: Other* symptoms may also be pointing to depression, not sadness. Do you care less about hobbies or socializing (an extrovert turned introvert)? Are you laying the guilt on yourself for situations that weren't your fault?
- *D: Decide* on alternatives to pulling back from life. What would you want to do if you weren't down in the dumps? For 30 minutes a day, even if takes your last ounce of energy, do one thing on your list of things you like to do. Switch your focus from feeling crappy to how you want to feel. What is that person feeling, doing, eating, thinking, and saying? How does that person look? Do small things to bring that person to life.

I will close out this chapter with this: If you're in the grips of depression, see a therapist, see a therapist, see a therapist. I can't say that enough. And when you go, take your journal notes with you. Life can get really hard, but it's never impossible. You can come out of this!

Time to celebrate!

By now, you're familiar with the "Triumph" pages, so head there and write yourself a thank-you note. Express gratitude for the lessons you have learned, your imperfections, your growth, your willingness to forgive, for being vulnerable, for facing the hardest parts of your story. And, most of all, for being *you*. Or simply write out whatever is in your heart at this moment.

SCIENCE SAYS...

"Depression is a common illness worldwide, with more than 264 million people affected."

—GBD 2017 Disease and Injury Incidence and Prevalence Collaborators. [2018]. "Global, regional, and national incidence, prevalence, and years lived with disability for 354 diseases and injuries for 195 countries and territories, 1990–2017: a systematic analysis for the Global Burden of Disease Study 2017. *The Lancet.* DOI

34

RESTORING WORK-LIFE HARMONY

- Is it difficult to create harmony between work and private life?

- What must occur so that your life and work support each other?

Taking time to live life will only inspire your work.

—Unknown

Have you ever felt like a circus elephant trying to balance on a ball? Staying steady and not falling off, well . . . that's the real challenge. There is give-and-take with everything in life, and the scale is usually tilted more to one side than the other. The same holds true for work and personal life. The more you attempt to balance them, to keep things equal, the more you realize it's nearly impossible. And there's this constant underlying feeling that you are always sacrificing one for the other.

What you're really in search of is harmony—that just-right combination (that sweet spot) between work and home. While the debate continues over whether you can have it all, work-life harmony is the happy medium where you can at least have your *slice* of the pie.

Work-life disharmony

When your professional and personal life don't mesh—they clash rather than co-existing—life gets very messy. You are pulled in every direction. It's a sign of work-life disharmony. The discord can lead to real aches and mental side effects. It can manifest in your body as neck and shoulder tension, back pain, headaches, stomach problems, irritability, and sheer exhaustion. As if that wasn't enough, trying to keep it all together can cut your sleep short, which usually means quality of sleep goes out the window. Sleep deprivation can also snowball into anxiety, depression, cardiovascular disease, heart disease, heart attacks, and strokes. A rift between pleasure and business can surely leave you feeling sick and tired.

H.A.R.M.O.N.Y

Restoring work-life harmony requires striking the right chord. Although emails, text messages, and work laptops have unofficially extended accessibility to 24 hours, 7 days a week, you can still orchestrate a meeting of the minds between work and your personal life such that the two don't create a sour note. *But how do you do it?*

H: Have focus and manage your time. That doesn't mean keeping tabs on the number of hours spent working versus personal time; remember, you are striving for harmony, not balance.

The point is to use your time wisely. Doing so lessens the competition between work and life and protects my me-time at the end of the work tunnel.

A: An active social life is also a good indicator of how well you are maintaining work-life harmony. If you can't remember when you last went out or met up with friends or loved ones, you might be overworking at the expense of missing milestones and special events. Set a goal to socialize at least once a week with people who uplift you and let you unwind. There is truth in the adage "All work and no play makes life dull."

R: Resist taking work home unless it rewards you with more happiness. If it looks like work, feels like work, and sounds like work, should you leave it at work? It depends. Work-life harmony requires a little flexibility. Sometimes you'll have to roll up your sleeves and give more at work for more personal time later; just promise yourself not to make it a habit. To enjoy more fruit from your labor, checking an email, answering a phone call, or responding to a text message after the whistle blows is a trade-off. But do proceed with caution, because these seemingly minor tasks can prevent you from recharging and place a strain on your mental health.

M: Make room for yourself at home and work. If your work demands that you keep everything that shapes your personal life separate from work, you're only living part-time—the evenings and maybe weekends. I've done it and felt miserable. A large part of work-life harmony is bringing what makes you feel good about you, what empowers you, and what motivates you into the office with you. It can be as simple as taking a few minutes during lunchtime for a brief meditation or journaling. Another thought is arranging your work and, if possible, your work environment to reflect you. For example, find a place to post a daily positive affirmation. Perhaps you and the team can come to a consensus on a couple of essential oil fragrances to lift the office mood. The main takeaway: It's important to love what you do; otherwise, harmony will fall flat.

O: Opting for excellence over perfection is a hot tip for work-life harmony. You are not going to have 365 perfect days any year, no matter how well you plan. Trying to walk such a tightrope defies work-life harmony. Do yourself a huge favor; cut yourself some slack, and set more obtainable goals. When you focus on excellence instead of perfection, you'll feel more accomplished because you'll have more checks in the success column. When wisdom whispers "Be perfectly imperfect," listen to that voice.

N: Nutritious eating is another key to striking better work-life harmony. With all the deadlines and high expectations, it's easy to place your well-being on the back burner. Fueling your body with healthier foods can mean the difference between having the stamina and health to achieve professional and personal goals or not. Pack a lunch and take a few minutes away from your desk to enjoy it. It keeps you in control over what you eat and ultimately helps you eat healthier.

Y: Your physical fitness is a great outlet to cope with the added pressure to do more faster and with less personal time. The survival of the *fittest* is applicable to creating work-life harmony. Exercise helps release pent-up stress, which is germane to being both happier and more productive. Refer back to the "Get up and Move" and "Fitness Is a Lifestyle" Prescriptions for a refresher.

Switching from personal to work mode shouldn't be a "hard no" when it comes to all the things you love. Find creative ways to integrate work and life that'll leave you in perfect harmony—I know I told you not to strive for perfection, but the word works well here, *ha-ha.*

You can't truly be
considered successful
in your business life
if your home life is
in shambles.

—**Zig Ziglar**

PRESCRIPTION 34

For Restoring Work-Life Harmony

For a happier ending, abandon the unproductive pursuit of the impossible work-life balance. Instead, strive for *what's possible*; find harmony between the two. It does exist!

Arrange your life to accommodate your work, and adapt your work to embrace aspects of your personal life—a melody that will leave you pleased about what you're doing in the office and at home. On that note, compose your thoughts (use the guide below) to make peace between your professional and your personal life.

What features of your personal life have a positive influence on your work?

Which ones make your work life more challenging?

How can you incorporate those positive things more often during work?

What can you change to lessen the negative effects of the more challenging aspects of your personal life on your work?

What features of your work life have a positive influence on your personal life?

Which ones make your personal life more challenging?

How can you incorporate those positive things more often in your personal life?

What can you change to reduce the negative effects of the more challenging aspects of your work life on your personal life?

Happiness

35

MAKE A
YOU-TURN

- Are you feeling off track in your life?

- Do you need to veer your life in a new direction?

> Rowing harder doesn't help
> if the boat is headed in the
> wrong direction.
>
> **—K. Ohmae**

Have you ever been driving around and felt like you were headed in the wrong direction but were hesitant to turn around? So you kept going, hoping to see landmarks that would reassure you that you were on the right path—even though your gut instinct was telling you that you weren't. Eventually, a course correction was at hand and you made a U-turn—a change in direction—to get back on the right road to reach your destination. Similarly, on life's voyage, sometimes a You-turn—a change in direction toward what is right for you in the present moment—is imminent to avoid hitting a dead end and to live your best life.

It's a 180-degree turn

We are creatures of habit, but I believe you can teach an old dog new tricks. Instead of digging in your heels and sticking to a path you feel comfortable with—despite knowing it's not right for you—use that stamina to turn your life around. It's okay to feel afraid of changing course. It's common to fear the unknown or fear making another wrong turn, and it can paralyze people from shifting direction. Don't be that person. It's like when a wheel is stuck in mud; you keep trying to accelerate in hopes of gaining traction, but you actually lose traction. You know you're not getting anywhere, but it's easier to continue spinning wildly than to put the car in neutral, get out, and push it out of the muddy path. You know it's going to be hard to get out of the deep groove, you're right about that, but the hard things are often the most worthwhile.

When you do decide to do a one-eighty, forget naysayers and forget what they say or think of your choices. (Remember the "For a Positive Mindset" Prescription?) No explanation is necessary if you're following a healthy decision of the heart. We all should be grateful for the chance to make a You-turn—so long as our choices don't shut the door on our passion and purpose.

Lights, Camera, Action!

Being center stage has always been exhilarating to me. And if I must say so myself, acting was one of my natural talents that only required a little fine-tuning. Each time I had the opportunity to step in front of an audience, I felt fireworks explode inside of me. I daydreamed of a career in theater, but the truth is my academics outperformed the standing ovations from my theater appearances. Against my own wishes, I pursued a career that aligned with high expectations and fewer disappointed looks. After all, don't we all assume that smart kids become doctors instead of actors? That may be the perception, but it isn't a fact.

Even though I'm proud of my success as a doctor, I still feel unaccomplished. Something has always been missing—I'm missing the curtain call. After a long delay, I'm a bundle of nerves, but I am making a You-turn to get back in front of the lights and camera to take action. I am launching my own internet television series, and the plan is to pitch it to national networks. This will be a win for me and you!

Now is the time

Have you ever put off something you wanted because of social pressure? Or because you believed it would just be easier to take the road *most* traveled? When you don't feel good about your life and it's not going the way you want, treading a new route is likely the breath of fresh air you need to revive a stagnant existence. The transformation might be a major one, like a change in lifestyle, attitude, career, or your social circle. Or it might be a minor one, like volunteering or adjusting things to be slightly different. The point is, if you're sick and tired of being sick and tired, make the You-turn.

Take a risk

Are you saying to yourself, "I'm not a risk-taker?" I once read that safety is an illusion, which would mean that continuing down the same wrong path is possibly the biggest risk.

You hold the key to turn your life around. The butterflies in your stomach will disappear when you build a more purposeful life. It's time to make a move and release any guilt for taking the road that's most gratifying for you at this moment in your life.

It's never too late to get back on track

At any age, it's okay to change your mind and make a shift to put your life back on track. Do not let second-best become your finest and final debut. No matter how hard you try, you will never be able to convince yourself that this was supposed to be your journey's end.

One day
your life
will flash
before your eyes.
Make sure
it's worth

watching.

—G. Way

PRESCRIPTION

For Making a You-Turn

If you haven't felt totally alive for a while and you're living halfheartedly, challenge yourself to fix your life. You *do* have the strength within you to get out of any rut. It's not up to someone else to save you. No one is coming. I know, because I wished for that too. I had to be my own hero, and so can you. The first step is the hardest: Become clear about what you do and do not want. How? Julia Cameron's *Morning Pages* is a brilliant engine for clarity and confidence.

As the title conveys, *Morning Pages* are done first thing in the morning. The reason for choosing this time of day is, according to Cameron, because the "veil of the ego is the thinnest." Journal three pages of longhand, stream-of-conscious writing. When you write in longhand, you are more emotionally engaged and present. There are no hard-and-fast rules except to fill *all three pages*. Don't overthink it; simply put down whatever thoughts cross your mind. Repeat this *every* morning. Initially, you may wonder if it's working, but if you make it part of your daily routine, you'll be surprised what you can (and will) discover about yourself.

When I prepare to do my own *Morning Pages* exercise, I begin with meditation and aromatherapy to sets the mood for my stream-of-conscious writing. I allot 20 to 30 minutes for the practice. That adds up to mean the first hour of my day is devoted to self-care. I pour time into myself so that I can have something to share with the world for the rest of the day.

If this concept feels a bit out there and you're unsure how to start, here is one of my own *Morning Pages* entries. I like the way blogger Shelby Abrahamsen put it: "Write, and the truth will fall out of your pen." Try starting with this:

If I release _____, which no longer suits me, I can make room for_____, which would bring me joy.

CHANGE YOUR PERSPECTIVE

- How's the worst thing the best thing that's ever happened to you?

- Does your present perspective on life align with your aspirations?

When life gets blurry,
adjust your focus.

—Unknown

A significant instance where you have the power to change your life is through your perspective. You have the authority to challenge it. Is this the number 6 or an upside-down number 9? When you see W, do you see the letter *W* or the letter *M*? It all depends on how you look at it, right? Where you stand alters your viewpoint. This doesn't only apply to numbers and letters; it also applies to life.

Changing the window through which you view the world changes your reality. It pulls the curtains back on new possibilities, but it also can lift the shades to reveal that what you've been looking for has been right in front of you the whole time—you merely needed a different field of vision. Would having a different perspective than the one you already have benefit you?

When I was a kid, I would sneak and put on my mother's glasses (I had to hurry because she was afraid I would break them). I'm not sure why I wanted to wear her glasses; they made everything around me blurry. But for my mother, those same glasses made things crystal clear. Changing the lens through which you view experiences opens another angle from which to see life, because there is rarely only one perception. Try metaphorically "taking the glasses off"—or putting them on—to clarify that your best life isn't as elusive (or blurry) as may seem.

The forest through the trees
If you truly want to live a richer, more fulfilling life that embodies your full potential, every now and again you will

need to adjust your focus. When you are faced with challenges, instead of allowing them to monopolize your time, damage your self-esteem, or take up permanent residence in your most valuable space—your mind and thoughts—take a step back. With the right lens, you can refresh your outlook and bring life into a better view.

Be open to a more panoramic picture that widens your frame of mind instead of magnifying your shortcomings. I've learned a lot from zooming in or out (figuratively) to see the wealth of possibilities available to me. It is life-changing to witness the dawn breaking on darkness by simply gaining a new perspective.

Different stages have different perspectives

The landscape appears different depending on whether you're at the beginning, middle, or nearing the end of a dilemma. From experience, it's tough to have an optimistic outlook in the beginning because your thoughts at that point are usually flooded with worry, stress, and fear. Your judgment is clouded and you can't visualize a way out of the situation. That's when you can remind yourself that you're still standing. There has been tough stuff before—divorce, unemployment, bankruptcy, domestic violence, poor health—that didn't take you out. This won't either. You can decide to see past the worst of things to zero in on the best.

Your power stance

Opposition can be a chance to take your power stance. If Stevie Wonder, Ray Charles, or Helen Keller had treated their blindness as an unbridgeable handicap, the world would have sadly missed out on legendary musicians and a prolific author. Instead, they saw and approached life differently, extraordinarily differently. They focused their inner eye on seeing life with powerful, lucid, and colorful vision. They saw hope, and you can too, if you change your perception.

There are
always flowers
for those who
want to see

them.

—Henri Matisse

PRESCRIPTION

For a Change in Perspective

Give this prescription your undivided attention. If it initially feels uncomfortable, move through it at a pace you're more comfortable with. Remember, this is *your* journey—you have control over your progress.

As we dive deeper each week, working through your transformational prescriptions won't necessarily get easier, but the reward of unlocking your life's potential will help drive away unsettled emotions. Like training for a marathon or any sports activity, putting in time and effort is necessary. These exercises will change how you look at situations, circumstances, and people, which will elevate the platform on which you live your life. For this Prescription, you'll need a separate piece of paper, a journal, or find some space on the pages in the back of this book.

1. Reflect on a situation you found unpleasant. Try to recall as many details as possible (e.g., your feelings, what other things were happening in your life, who was involved, who supported you, how you felt inhibited by it), and journal as much as you can about the event.

2. If there were other persons involved, attempt to tell the story from their perspective. If not, make a genuine effort to look at the event from various angles—change your lens.

3. If you encountered this opposition again, how could you approach it differently, and how would approaching it in this manner result in a better outcome?

Your perception
determines
what you believe
and how you inevitably
permit things
to affect

you.

—Anonymous

THE AUTHENTIC YOU

- Do you hold back on your own truth to be accepted and fit in?

- Are you pursuing who you think you should be or who you are?

The authentic self is the SOUL
made visible.

—Sarah Ban Breathnach

It can feel like a pretty sizable chore to express your authentic self when at every turn you are being coaxed to be and act like someone else. Betraying yourself—not living according to your heart—is one of the most unhealthy acts you can commit. You censor who you are in order to be accepted. Beneath the facade, you feel like crap because something is all wrong, and you know it. That nagging feeling is coming from the *authentic you*. Being forced to live below the radar hardly seems fair, especially when you have been put here to leave your unique watermark.

What does inauthentic vs. authentic living feel like?
When I wasn't living authentically, I felt a constant internal struggle between the life I really wanted and the life I thought I had to live. I was mentally and spiritually exhausted. It took an enormous amount of energy just to get out of bed and put my feet on the floor. I was unengaged and disconnected from my own life.

Everything was a task. It wasn't until I made the conscious decision to live my authentic life that I felt alive, again—what joy! Discovering what it meant to be authentic opened up my world, my life. I became attuned to me. I no longer needed a stamp of approval to live my life because within my purpose I already, naturally, had permission.

A quick test of your authenticity is to ask yourself this: *If it takes away from who you are, why are you doing it?*

Authenticity is the author of a healthy you

The freedom to show up as the person you were created to be is its own reward. Sorry to say, it's not seen as such until you are coerced into abandoning what makes you, *you*. But it is the genuine version of you, the one that isn't pretending, that has the most to share with others and the most to give to yourself. The real you also has the pleasure of living without regret.

Authenticity is the author of a healthy mind, a healthy life, and a healthy you.

How will you know it's your authentic you?

It is the uninhibited you who emerges when no one is taking note. It is the most honest expression of yourself, without modifications made under pressure, influence, or intimidation. It is when "yes" or "no" is a decision because it is in line with your purpose, not because it is the path of least resistance. It is refusing to wear what does not fit your life. It is the bare-naked, purest form of you.

The measure of authenticity

Authenticity divulges your innate worth and shields it from being devalued—even by you. And when you're hold your true self in high regard, you won't waste any more time going along to just get along.

What is the true measure of being genuine?

- You are willing to move forward even when you are afraid.

- You are concerned less about the opinions of others and more about yours.
- You become the author of your own story.
- Your life is enough.
- You understand that challenges are just built-in pauses.
- You are immediately aware of inauthentic living.

Getting to know the real you

Being yourself means cultivating the seeds that are already planted within you. Give yourself the right soil and time to grow and you'll blossom into your true self. Every day, I look forward to uncovering and learning more about the authentic me. I've opened myself to a lifetime of wonder and opportunity, and I know you'll have the same vigor for your own life when you refuse to live any way other than authentically!

Introducing your authentic self to the world may be more involved than just waking up and "you doing you," especially if you have veered off track for fear of judgment. Reconnect spiritually, mentally, and emotionally. Be kind and empathetic toward yourself. Release guilt and shame. Pray for guidance and wisdom. Be confident about what you believe. You'll get there—I know it. Everyone has a story, so lean into yours. Make sure you tell your own life story and never trade it for someone else's—an original is priceless.

One of the greatest
tragedies in life is to
lose your authentic self
and accept the version
of you that is expected
by everyone

else.

—K. L. Toth

PRESCRIPTION

For Becoming the Authentic You

Who is the authentic you? It seems like a straightforward question, but it's a surprisingly difficult question to answer. And until you develop a clear picture of the authentic you, it will be difficult to construct your road map to the life you desire and deserve. Let me help you do the work; take some time and use the following questions to guide you.

1. Write a short bio describing who you are today, at this very moment.

2. Read and then reread your bio. Then write a short bio describing the you that you want to be.

3. Reflect on your two bios. Write down the differences between the two.

4. What are some small measures you can take today to move toward the authentic you?

You've come so far. Time to celebrate!

You should be so proud of yourself for welcoming healing, better health, and a good measure of happiness into your life. It's for a wonderful cause: *You*. What acts of kindness can you do for yourself to show appreciation for this moment? Jot them down in the "Triumph" section, then pick one and do it!

SCIENCE SAYS...

"People who scored higher on a measure of authentic living reported greater happiness, more positive emotions, and higher self-esteem than people who reported being less authentic."

—Matthew A. Wood et al. "The Authentic Personality: A Theoretical and Empirical Conceptualization and the Development of the Authenticity Scale," *Journal of Counseling Psychology*, 2008, 55(3): 385–99

REDISCOVER YOU

- What passions have you given up in the busyness of life?

- What was your BIG dream?

The privilege of a lifetime is to become who you truly are.

—**Carl Jung**

It *is* conceivable to lose touch with yourself. How's that possible? With the many roles and relationships that are a part of your life, it's easy to become wrapped up in everyone and everything except yourself. It may even be a welcomed distraction. But a loss of identity—an indifference about who you are and what's important to you—is not the greatest feeling. It is joyless, confusing, and daunting. And worse, being estranged from yourself and not loving your life can make you feel like an imposter, a fake. If you're growing distant from yourself, there's no better time than now, right now, to stop skimming the surface of your life and become reacquainted with what turns you on, with what gets you all hot and bothered.

You will find your way
First things first: Either recognize that you're lost or that you are right where you need to be in the moment. Before questioning every aspect of your life, you won't always know exactly what you are doing with your life—*breathe*, that's normal. That feeling of being lost is you figuring out if you are moving further from or closer to the *you* you've dreamt about. Keep in mind that a newfound you can be wonderful. You *will* find your way; the sun always rises in the east and sets in the west.

Listen to the beat of your own drum
Soul-searching reveals the road map to yourself. When you look inward, you get back in touch with your own story so you can rediscover what it is that fills *you* with jubilance.

Just because you have lost sight of yourself, fulfillment, meaning, and passion for life aren't gone forever—you just have to reclaim them. Be willing to be vulnerable in order to hit upon what really makes your heart sing.

Listen to the beat of your own drum and march in sync to *your* beautiful music. It will bring you sheer pleasure, so much so that you'll inspire others to do the same.

Go back to the start

A big part of finding myself was admitting I was lost and pinpointing why. My narrow definition of success convinced me that life was great until I could no longer be persuaded. Even with the job, status, and lifestyle, I still felt like I was living the wrong life. If you feel like there's got to be more to life, then there *is* more.

Having trouble finding your internal compass? Retrace your steps. Go back to where you lost your footing. What were the circumstances—pregnancy, marriage or divorce, health challenges, a promotion denied, fear (it's constantly rearing its ugly head)? Knowing where you think you got lost in the first place is the surest way to find yourself again.

You're too valuable to stay lost

Life is ever changing, and so are you. Even though you might be unsure about the direction your compass needle is pointing, you are en route. The joy of rediscovering yourself as an individual—not in your role as a parent, spouse, sibling, friend, child, employee, or employer—is one of life's most sought-after treasures. You're far too valuable to stay lost forever. And you won't, but it does not mean you won't get lost again.

Sometimes when you
lose your way,
you find

Yourself.

—Mandy Hale

PRESCRIPTION

For Rediscovering Yourself

At some point in life, most of us get side-tracked. Our lives can seem as if we've taken a wrong turn—we wonder how we got "here"— which feels downright scary. If we aren't careful, we can become isolated and depressed. But before going there, there's an upside: We do not have to remain lost. It's time to reconnect you with yourself.

What do you feel is missing from your life? When do you remember last having it?

What happened to create this big hole in your life?

Name three things that would make you want to leap from bed with excitement? What do you need to do to make room for them in your life?

What's something you've put off that would make your life more satisfying? Outline the steps to make it happen—manifest it.

39

REIMAGINE YOUR LIFE

- Have you lost that spark—that enthusiasm—for life?

- How will you write the next chapter in your life?

A man sooner or later discovers
that he is the master-gardener of
his soul, the director of his life.

—James Allen

There was time when your dreams weren't so far-fetched. You believed you could *be* whoever you wanted to be and *do* whatever you wanted to do. You closed your eyes and imagined it, and you believed—somehow—that you could bring your imagination to life. The sky was the limit (if there was one). You resisted being held back by what you did not have or who you did not know. You were flexible in your thinking, potential, and behavior. You gave your dreams power. It's how they came true. *Reimagine that!*

Once upon a time . . .

I dreamed of being a queen (thus my collection of tiaras—which I actually received from my participation in piano recitals, but that's my little secret), a professional ice skater, an actress, a mother, a wife, a world-renowned pianist, the president—the possibilities were endless and only inhibited by my imagination.

The sweet innocence of childhood could not be caged by boundaries. But one day, it happened. I can't recall the age when I stopped dreaming or toned my dreams down. The age when I started fitting my life into a box, a box that left some of my dreams dangling on the outside.

Dream out loud

Who defines what's possible for you? Only I can make such big decisions for me. And I hope that's true for you too. When everything in your mind and body is telling you to go for it, *go for it.* Dream out loud. Unless you do the things you think you cannot do, you will never know that you can do them.

Dreams are fuel

Where did you leave off in your dreams? It's not too late to pick up the torch and activate your purpose again. If someone says it's outlandish, ignore them. And if *you're* the naysayer, stop that negative thinking in its tracks. (*Hint:* look at the "For a Positive Mindset" Prescription.) If you stop saying "no," then the universe will begin saying "yes." Go after the life you've imagined (or reimagined) as if your life depends on it, because—Lord knows—it kind of does.

Everyone was born with an imagination. Dreams are the fuel for the life that was meant to be yours from the moment you took your first breath.

Pair your dreams with a leap of faith

Life has the tendency to become stale when what you are living toward is outdated (or has reached its expiration date). However, if you're up for re-envisioning life and pairing your dreams with a leap of faith, the life you wish to live is yours for the taking. There will be no shortage of effort on your part, but the trade-off is enjoying a happier and healthier life.

What do I dream from here?

Dreaming is how you reimagine fulfillment in your life, because life rarely goes according to plan—single and childless in the city was certainly an unexpected turn of events for me. Because your backdrop is always changing—married, divorced, children, empty-nester, working, retired, illness—you must invariably be rethinking and asking: *What do I dream from here?*

"Re-dream"

Spin around while letting out a *whew*, because you get to do something amazing: You get to reimagine your life. Or, as Lauren Selfridge phrased it, you get to "re-dream." Seriously, stand up and spin and shout! If it feels scary, it should. This is your pivotal moment, the moment you dream again. I can only imagine where they'll take you!

Your imagination
is your preview
of life's coming

attractions.

—**Albert Einstein**

PRESCRIPTION

For Reimagining Your Life

Welcome to one of the best days of your life! Today is the day you release restrictions you've placed on yourself so that you're free to live the life you imagine. Before you dive in, pause and take a deep breath, then exhale and lift your arms openly (remember what you've learned about breathing thus far).

For this prescription, allow yourself time to reflect upon your heartfelt desires. Don't rush; remember to take a few deep breaths. After you have given serious thought about the next chapter of your life, write it out and create a visual. It will bring clarity and add substance to your dream, making it feel tangible and attainable.

Part 1

1. If someone performs an internet search for you, what are the relevant key words?
2. What qualities and talents do you choose to highlight?
3. What do you want to accomplish in this season of your life?
4. What does a fresh start look like to you?
5. What distractions or responsibilities are preventing you from your ideal life?
6. How can you balance obligations with your dreams? You may not have an answer right now, but feel free to brainstorm.

Part 2

Next, create a vision board that reflects what you want to accomplish and attract to your life. Don't make this complicated—gather pictures and thumbtack them to a corkboard or even glue them to paper. Write a plan to achieve each goal. When your board is finished, place it somewhere you'll be able to see it daily. Now, start your journey. Refuse to leave this world with dreams buried inside of you; absolutely refuse.

40

DON'T WORRY . . .
CHOOSE JOY

- What is one thing you can do each day to become joy-centered?

- When is the last time you jumped and shouted for joy?

Joy; the kind of happiness that
doesn't depend on what happens.

—David Steindl-Rast

There's nothing pretentious about choosing joy, but it can feel that way until you understand joy is not about a feeling; it's about how you choose to live your life no matter what. It doesn't mean living a lie—it is not an act or denial—actually, it's accepting life as it is. I know joy doesn't always make perfect sense, but neither does life.

Choosing joy means . . .

The nice thing about joy is you don't have to chase it—you simply choose it. It's omnipresent, all around you (and me). Joy is lit from within. If you don't know what you're looking for, it can be easily missed. Most of the time you have to look below the surface to find joy. Sometimes is at the third-eye level—in how you perceive the world.

Dog-ear this page for a reminder of what it means to choose joy.

Choosing joy means . . .

- counting your blessings instead of keeping score of your losses.
- accepting life unconditionally.
- believing in life after hurt and disappointments.
- focusing on the present moment.
- lowering your guard enough to open your heart to others.
- exercising faith in times of challenges.
- intentionally seeking the positive.
- living with high hopes in spite of fear.
- being grateful.
- trusting God's will for your life.

- deciding your responses to situations.
- prioritizing emotional well-being.
- affirming who you are without validation from others.
- giving forgiveness and not taking it back.
- cherishing your joy and not allowing it to be taken from you.
- inviting into your life what serves you and letting go of what doesn't.
- acknowledging that it is a real choice.

You're right; choosing joy isn't always easy—then again, what in life worth having is easy? I am sure there are things not on this list that fill you with joy. Each of us has the responsibility of defining what joy means on a personal level.

Joy is the happiness you choose

Joy is a divine privilege and a decision you make—it's the happiness you choose. Unlike some, I don't believe that happiness is a second cousin to joy; no surprise there, since I used the word *happiness* in the title of my book. You should experience and enjoy them both every day. Neither is enough without the other. The contentedness that's implicit in joy is the impetus to encounter more moments of happiness in your life. I've found that joy—described by Danielle Laporte as the "fiber of your soul"—guides me in the direction of where happiness is more attainable and not as easy to crush because it's less externally inspired.

Joy is not exclusive

Are you having a little trouble finding your joyful self? I remember when I first understood the concept of joy. I was watching an interview in which a woman was discussing the loss of her husband. His death was unexpected, and what made it even more tragic was that she was pregnant with their child. Despite the hardship, she explained that in her time of turmoil and loss, she made the choice to live joyfully. I could feel her joy *atop* her pain, and then it hit me. Joy is *not* exclusive of our circumstances. There were times in my life when being sad seemed organic, but something gave me peace. That something, I realized, was *joy*.

Jump and shout for joy

No matter what happens, know that joy is yours to have and to keep. And choosing joy can mean all the difference in your world—jump and shout that joy is your choice and your personality type.

Joy does not simply
happen to us.
We have to choose joy
and keep choosing
it every

day.

—Henri Nouwen

PRESCRIPTION

For Choosing Joy

Now that you know joy isn't just for the lucky few but for everyone—including you—how do you encourage and nurture joy in your life? It's not as difficult as you might think, especially once you discover it in the simple places, loving relationships, your laughter, the rain, or just holding open a door for someone.

Let's bring more joy into your life. The first step is to *stop waiting to be joyful*. Find it in ordinary, everyday things. Start discovering joy by completing this short exercise. You can write here or in a journal.

1. Define what choosing joy means for you.

2. What are five ways you experience joy on a daily basis?

3. Describe the last time you felt joyous. How old were you? Who was there? What did it feel like? Why did the experience make you joyful?

4. Start and end each day on a joyful note. I am joyful for _____ (focus internally).

5. Commit one random act of kindness weekly for four weeks. Keep it simple, and it doesn't need to cost you anything. For example, share a home-cooked meal, leave a positive message on a desk, or simply smile at someone who looks bored or unhappy.

41

DOUBLE-DARE YOU TO DO IT DIFFERENTLY

- What do you need to do differently to make your life happier?

- Are you following your curiosity or taking the safe road?

If you always do what you always did, you will always get what you always got.

—Albert Einstein

I dare you to:

- Respond differently.
- Adopt a different attitude.
- Think differently.
- Dream differently.
- Believe differently.
- Love differently.
- Go after life differently.

I dare you—no, I double-dare you—to do it all *differently*!

Blending in is so yesterday

My mother cautioned me about being a follower—it's best to be the ringleader in your group of one. Blending in is so yesterday—be the yellow, pink, red, green, polka-dot umbrella in a swarm of black ones. Life is much too short to *not* venture off the beaten path. If you want to shake things up, become curious enough to approach life differently—you don't have another shot at life, but you have a shot at making this one your best.

It's time!

Do you agree it takes more than wishing things were different for them to actually be different? If you are less than thrilled with your life, feel like something is missing, or have an itch to try something new, it's a sign it is time to do life differently.

Make your world go round

There's definitely a sense of reassurance—whether it's real or false—in familiarity, I will give you that much. But ask yourself: Why settle for run-of-the-mill when you could live a life that makes your world go round?

Taking the first step to change things up may cause some butterflies in your stomach, clammy hands, a racing heart, or broken sleep. Channel that nervous energy into taking action to live your unlived life—the part you won't entertain because it requires you to consider life in a different light.

I've been there, in that uncomfortable moment of do I or don't I break the mold. In fact, writing this very book is an example of me doing life differently and opening up to a new space in the world. I procrastinated because I wasn't sure if it would be well received. But then again, the reason for writing the book isn't to be well received, it's to unlock the path to my true potential. And in truth, writing it has been the key to sending out vibrations that are in tune with what I desire for my next chapter of life.

You have the power

Here's an idea: Act as though you have the power to turn possibilities into realities. Why? Because you *do* have the power!

Life resets when you dare to live it differently. If you want to lose weight but dieting isn't working—remember my earlier Prescriptions on health—then do something different. Maybe you want to change your status from single to being in a relationship, but your daily routine consists of little besides driving to work and back home. Then do something differently. I've struggled with that one myself; let me know what you come up with. If you want to open your own business but are too busy to write a business plan—do something different. You have heard it a thousand times: When you want something different, you've gotta *do* some different things. There's no way around it.

When I challenged my status quo and let go of the traditional image of a doctor, something amazing occurred—and best of all, I got unstuck. At first I had concerns about my colleagues' and families' opinions. The funny thing is, most people are not that focused on you or what you're doing, and the people who are, well, they're your secret admirers. They may not admit it, but do not let them tell you any differently.

If you dare . . .

I dared, and I'm becoming what I had set out to become. I'm putting my unique twist on the art of medicine as an author, a guest on podcasts, and my soon-to-be-live talk show and meditation series. I'm over-the-moon excited. If I can do it, so can you. I double-dare you to live life with imagination (flip back to the "Reimagine Your Life" Prescription)—and watch it change! What great things are waiting for you when you decide to do life differently?

Just when you think
you know something,
you have to look at
in another way.
Even though it may
seem silly or wrong,
you must

try.

—John Keating

PRESCRIPTION 41

For Daring to Do It Differently

Ready to get out of your rut? Do I hear a *heck yes*? Well then, huddle up for a different game plan. Write down two areas in your life you feel passionately about doing differently. For each, answer the following:

Why is this important to you now?

What prior actions have you taken to bring about change in this area?

Why haven't you been successful at achieving the results you wanted?

Define success as it relates to this area in your life.

What can you do differently to create success this time?

What are your challenges?

What resources will you need?

Identify one or two people who support you and keep you accountable.

How much time weekly will you devote to working toward creating this change in your life?

What is the timeframe to accomplish your goal?

You've achieved something awesome again, time to celebrate!

I really love these breaks to celebrate and acknowledge your perseverance. It was a suggestion from a focus group organized by my editor—I must give credit where it is due.

This celebration is a bit different than others (in keeping with the idea of doing things differently, of course). I know our smartphones can take some beautiful pictures, but consider a photoshoot with a photographer. It would be a lovely way to capture your transformation and the new energy radiating from within. Put together an inspiration board of photos (you can tape them on the "Triumph" pages) and arrange a meeting with a photographer. If cost is an issue, ask a close friend to help.

42 IT'S TIME TO F.L.Y.

- How do you express self-love toward yourself?

- Do you have the heart to put your needs above others?

Love is the great miracle cure.
Loving ourselves works miracles
in our lives.

—Louise Hay

Place your seat-back in the upright position and fasten your seatbelt, because it's time to F.L.Y.: First, Love Yourself.

Self-love has been wrongly mistaken for selfishness, arrogance, and self-indulgence. I made this error myself, but the terms are *not* synonymous, not even in the smallest degree. Expressing patience, gentleness, and kindness toward yourself is not self-centeredness. If you're still on the fence about self-love, think about this way: If your bucket is empty, you have nothing to share with anyone, least of all yourself.

Even the airlines encourages self-love, they instruct you that in an emergency situation put on your oxygen mask before assisting others. This message re-emphasizes that you can better help others when you take care of yourself first. Safety aside, self-love keeps you from feeling depleted, empty, and resentful that your needs aren't a priority—especially to you.

Oxygen to your soul

Genuine self-love is *oxygen* to the soul—a basic human necessity. I equate it to a breath of fresh air that infuses you with the confidence to honor yourself as you are right now. It's grace that only you can extend to yourself.

Believe you deserve to be loved by you. Read that statement again. And then really *believe* you deserve to be loved by you. If needed, pause here to meditate (review the "Meditate Day and Night" Prescription). Take your time. This is *very, very* important. Because everyone needs to be loved by themselves.

Even though I knew I should love myself, I am not sure I always did. Taking a vow to love *me*, first and foremost,

changed my entire relationship, unapologetically and unequiv-
ocally, with myself and those I love—for the good. I cannot
be in a healthy relationship with anyone until I'm in one with
myself. I don't think it is much of a risk to say, neither can you.

Unconditional self-love

Living from a place of unconditional self-love can be hard—it
can feel like work. But the more you practice acts of self-appre-
ciation, they will become second nature. You'll want to bring
more of it into your life, and perhaps wonder how you ever
lived without it. Think of being sincerely sweet on yourself and
holding your *must-haves* in high regard as next-level happiness!

Be the example

Be the primary example of the love you are seeking. The more
you honor yourself, others will follow suit. People won't love
you more than you love yourself—it's too much to ask and
expect. The onus is upon you to teach them what loving you
looks like. Then again, you can only love someone as much
as you love yourself. Self-love raises the bar on being able to
spread true love.

Learn to F.L.Y.

First, Love Yourself. When you have a loving relationship with
yourself, it directly influences the way you "show up" in your
life, the image you project to the world, and your choices. Of

all the paths you must travel, the one to self-love will bring you enormous life satisfaction and fulfillment!

The best love story, ever

Self-love is the best love story you'll ever live! It should be one of your first introductions to true love. That magical feeling of being in love isn't reserved for couples. It comes from the way you express protectiveness, affection, and respect for yourself. At the very center of who you are is a reservoir of self-compassion and self-acceptance. Tap into it. It's a wonderful feeling to be absolutely fond of yourself—and there's not one selfish thing about it. It's actually wholesome to *swoon* over yourself.

You don't have to wait around for someone else to shower you with love. Believe that, y*ou got you!* Self-love is personal, but for starters think about forgiveness, physical activity, proper sleep, healthy nutrition, and affirmations. Enjoy every single ounce of your own tender loving self-care—be your forever valentine.

To love oneself
is the beginning
of a lifelong

romance.

—Oscar Wilde

PRESCRIPTION

For Learning to F.L.Y.

42

Do you have a daily self-love ritual? If not, adopt one. I approach my day with meditation and prayer. Taking a few minutes in the morning to supercharge my soul establishes a positive mindset as I set out to greet the day.

On most days, I fit in Pilates or cycling, affirmations, a healthy meal, and lots of laughs. I bring my day to a close by cleansing my face and aromatherapy. My skincare regimen takes only a few minutes, but it is so refreshing and renewing. It is a small reminder that is it important to take care of me! Self-love may seem a big concept and a bit vague, but you have to make it tangible for you. Find and do what makes you feel loved.

Get started

Enough talk; take action. Get in the habit of being the love you need. Write yourself some self-love prescriptions. Start with five self-love therapies. Keep them simple and doable. To help get the creative juices flowing, here are some of my doses of self-love:

- *Memorize a pick-me-up message.* Have a positive go-to cheer in mind to inspire yourself. When the day feels hectic, visualize cheering yourself on. I tell myself to be encouraged; it doesn't have to unfold according to my plans—maybe that's a good thing.

- *Say something kind.* You don't have to wait for a compliment; give yourself one. Say something nice. There's nothing wrong with acknowledging what makes you feel special—some days you have to create your own sunshine. I'll get you started: I'm so proud of you for the work you're doing on yourself. You're beginning to shine, and it's gorgeous!

- *Tap into your thoughts.* Carve out time to be still in your mind. Appreciate what you've accomplished each day. Don't forget to listen to your intuition to hear what your soul may desire.

- *Forgive yourself.* You've heard the saying "Don't go to bed angry." So be careful not to climb under the sheets with regret and heaviness. Apologize to yourself and let it go. This is in no way easy. If you need a refresher on this, go back to the Prescription on forgiveness.

- *Be good to your body.* Whether it's a brisk walk or stroll, Pilates, yoga, a run, or cycling, movement is good way to show your body, "I love you."

Celebrate your shine!

Making self-love a part of a daily routine is challenging for most of us. The more you do it, the more you'll appreciate all the goodness in your life. I'm sending you lots of love and warm wishes for your self-love journey. I hope you can feel the positive vibes. Before forging ahead, take a break to record a triumph or two. You deserve it!

43

YOU AREN'T REALLY STUCK

- What has you feeling stuck?

- What do you believe is missing in your life right now?

 At any given moment, you have
the power to say this is not
how the story is going to end.

—Christine Mason Miller

It may feel as though you have been stuck in the same place for what feels like an eternity, and no matter what you try, you cannot gain momentum. You are just going through the motions. Sounds familiar?

Being "stuck" is a deceptive boundary you have drawn around your potential. Being "stuck" is believing false limitations and buying into unsupported fear, both of which keep you out of commission. Breathe; you are not stuck, but feeling stuck can be very intimidating. It's immobilizing; I've been there, mostly when my life was out of harmony.

You're not stuck

You're not stuck in a career you don't enjoy. You can plan an exit strategy.

You're not stuck in an unhealthy relationship. You can love yourself enough to leave.

You're not stuck with being unhappy. You can choose to live happily ever after.

You're not stuck in a financial crisis. You can change your spending and saving habits.

You're not stuck in your home. You can book your next trip (or your first).

You're not stuck dreaming. You can bring your dreams to fruition.

You're not stuck feeling unwell. You can live a healthier lifestyle.

You're not stuck in the past. You can let go and move forward.

You're not stuck. You can decide to tell yourself a different story and believe it.

You get the picture, mental obstacles can make you feel like you are, but you *are not* stuck.

Stop wrestling with the unknowns

The question to answer is: *What has you thinking that you are in some sort of holding pattern—circling around and around and around?* Is there an obvious pink elephant in the room—a problem you know is there but refuse to acknowledge? Take it from someone who took that approach to no avail; the pink elephant doesn't disappear just because you do not confront it—it'll get bigger.

If you feel like you're not moving forward in life, could it be that you are spending far too much time and energy wrestling with all the unknowns? Surely that can put anyone in a slump. Your ducks won't always be in row, and a security net won't always be beneath you to break your fall. I've said it before in this book and I'm saying it again: *Take the leap of faith.*

The benefits of being stuck

Here is a twist you didn't see coming. You may be benefiting from alleging that you are stuck. It stunned me, too. Personal development author Blaz Kos wrote: "In comparison, the pain of being stuck is smaller than the pain of freeing yourself and doing something about it." That's profound. No judgment, but you cannot continue to choose being stuck because of financial security, what others will think, not wanting to be alone, or whatever else has you feeling jammed up. Come out from hiding and get unstuck!

Fear of the unknown

Fear is an emotion that keeps many of us—not just you—feeling stuck and unhealthily attached to unwanted situations. Fear doesn't necessarily mean you are trembling or your heart is racing. It implies that your circumstances have incapacitated you and your true purpose is at risk.

Fear is the culprit that has buried many dreams, but it is never too late to resurrect them! I just wanted to share that thought. If you need to, flip back to the Prescription for fear.

But how do you shake the feeling?

Another question to ask yourself: *What would make you feel unstuck?* That's where you need to start. Sometimes the way out of your rut is changing your mindset; other times it's standing up to a lingering issue, or maybe it's ending a fruitless relationship. Sometimes it's believing in your talents, and other times it's to stop making excuses. I had to change where I was spending my time, energy, and resources. And voilà! My life took off again!

You have to determine where it all went south in your mind *and* in your life. When you do, you can begin to shake that awful feeling of being stuck. To give you some comfort, please stop reading and say this loud and clear: *I am not stuck.*

Let that truth resonate. Say it over and over if it helps, but keep reading it or saying it until you have an "aha" moment.

When we feel stuck,
going nowhere—even
starting to slip
backward—we may
actually be backing up
to get a running

start.

—Dan Millman

PRESCRIPTION 43

For Becoming Unstuck

It's time to name your pink elephant! Tell me: What has you mentally trapped? If the bridge from where you are now to where you want to be is not clear and something always seems to be blocking you from taking the next step, identify what is making you feel stuck and plan to overcome it.

The first step in this process is knowing what you want. Some might know exactly what they want in their career, in their love life, in their next home, and so forth. Others might not be as certain; they just know they want to be happier than they are right now. Either way is a fine place to start.

Consider one thing that has you feeling stuck. Now turn it into a direct statement, beginning with "I'm not." Many affirmations urge you to repeat what you are, stating "I am." However, there's an equal amount of power in acknowledging what you are *not* experiencing. I'm not working on a job that I love. I'm not traveling as much as I want to. I'm not working out consistently. The idea is to have a balance between the two thoughts. Complete the following table. Bookmark this page, and come back as often as you need.

I AM NOT . . .	I AM . . .

The Five Whys

Once you've made your statement, get to the root cause. We'll do that by using "The Five Whys," developed by Sakichi Toyoda.

Start with your direct statement and then ask yourself why. Follow your response with another why and then another, until you can't go any further. You might not need all five whys, or you may need more. Here is an example:

1. Why am not traveling as much as I'd like? *Because I do not have the money.*

2. Why don't I have the money? *Because I am not saving any.*

3. Why am I not saving money? *Because I use it for retail therapy—buying shoes and purses.*

4. Why do I use money for retail therapy? *Because I can escape from my real problems.*

5. Why do I want to escape from my real problems? *Because I don't know where to get help.*

Now you try it with your own whys. Keep going until you feel you're at the root of the problem and you don't feel stuck!

You deserve a round of applause. Give yourself one!

SCIENCE SAYS...

"Sixty-nine percent of people feel trapped in the same old routine, and only 3 out of 10 people are happy with their lives."

—Source:
"Just three in 10 people feel happy with their lives,"
(The Telegraph, 22 January 2015)

LAUGH OUT LOUD (LOL)

- What are some things that make you laugh?

- What's something that made you double up with laughter?

Laughter is the fireworks
of the soul.

—Josh Billings

Laughing has been referred to as "internal jogging" because it has a similar impact on the body as moderate exercise, and that's no joke. *But* it's not an excuse to skip your workout—so don't even think about it! As you engage with the Prescription for this week, make sure you pause occasionally for comic relief.

When was the last time you had a deep belly laugh? I mean one where you nearly rolled on the floor and your eyes watered. Well, there is no time like the present: *Have one right now!* Smile, snicker, giggle, chuckle until you burst into laughter! It's okay if you're choosing to laugh instead of it being spontaneous—this is one of those times you can fake it until you're in stitches. A hearty laugh tickles the spirit and wakes up the soul. It's important to not take yourself so seriously; lighten up. When you can laugh at yourself, it takes the edge off life. It is a good reminder to not sweat the small—or big—stuff. Whatever hurdles you are facing, if you can still laugh, clearing them will be a lot easier.

A natural high

Turn that frown upside down and laugh out loud (LOL)! It's one of the best antidotes for a tough day. A dose of healthy cheerful laughter is natural medicine to release stress. It is a mood enhancer and a great way to regain perspective. Science has proven that the endorphins released as you laugh reduce chronic pain, improve emotional well-being, distance depression, and boost the way your immune system functions. All joking aside—laughter heals the mind, body, and soul.

The more you find reasons to laugh, the more happiness you will encounter and the less you'll let life's mishaps drag you down. Take a moment now to remember a few funny things that have happened, or imagine something silly that *could* happen. Then enjoy that smile and take note of the warmth it brings to your soul. Speaking of which, if you want to attract romance, a sourpuss is not going to win anyone over, no matter your gender. According to research, "women like jokey men, while men like women who laugh at their jokes." One more reason to relax and let out a chuckle.

LOL check-ins

When I laugh, it's a sign for me that everything will be alright. If you are sitting in my office waiting area, you are guaranteed to hear me laugh; it's one of the ways I check in with myself. If it has been a while since I've heard the sound of my laughter, it's a sign that I may be letting the task at hand get the best of me. It's a warning that I need to look within to see what's out of balance.

A good chuckle isn't limited to only good times—you have access to your funny bone 24/7! LOLing doesn't mean life is going smoothly—sometimes it's the contrary, and the laugh allows a much-needed release. Regardless, laughter elevates my mood. My patients tell me that hearing me laugh brightens their day! Maybe yours could brighten someone else's day too. It's a win-win, because laughter is contagious.

Although laughter doesn't erase actual issues, it is a pressure-relief valve that helps you manage them with a more positive mindset. (There's another reference to a previous Prescription—you've learned so much already!)

Schedule a laugh break

Laughter is mind therapy. It counteracts negativity. The benefits are so rewarding, I set my intentions to add a little humor to my life daily—you should too. Put a laugh session on the calendar the same way someone might plan to carry out their work-life responsibilities. Don't settle for just seeing if it'll happen naturally; make sure that it does happen, and whatever comes naturally can be a bonus.

I don't watch much television, but a couple times a week I tune into a sitcom or view a few minutes of stand-up comedy to get some giggles. I also schedule FaceTime with my toddler niece. She cracks me up with her "Hmm, no thanks" whenever I'm telling her to do something. Here are a few jokes that may make you crack a smile!

- Did you hear the one about the little mountain? *It's hill-arious!*
- Why do Dasher and Dancer love coffee? *Because they're Santa's star bucks!* (It's funny, get it? Ha-ha!)
- Becoming a vegetarian is a huge *missed steak.*

There's nothing like
the deep breaths
we take after
laughing a lot.
There's nothing in the
world like a stomach
that hurts for a good

reason.

—S. Chbosky

PRESCRIPTION

For Laughing Out Loud

Laughter is a universal language that needs no interpretation. No matter how you choose to do it, squeeze in some hearty chuckles—it's actually good for you!

What makes you giggle uncontrollably? Here's your chance to play doctor: Self-prescribe daily doses of laughter. Don't worry about the laugh lines; they're a small trade-off to feel more at ease. In fact, they are a badge of honor for a life full of joy, despite disappointments.

Call a friend who makes you laugh, flip through photos, watch a comedy, or just be a little silly. There's always laughter yoga—laughter exercises coupled with breathing techniques to train the body how to laugh without relying on jokes, fun stuff! It's a real thing! The point is to bring more laughter into your life—lighten the mood, turn on your sense of humor, or at least smile:

- Go to a funny movie (or watch videos) or read a funny book.
- Plan a monthly night out with friends who are a hoot.
- Take a silly selfie; laugh at yourself.
- Learn to tell a joke.
- Read a few jokes daily and share your favorite joke of the day.
- Create a poster board of things that make you laugh.

Okay, let's close this chapter with a good belly laugh . . .

Have you heard about the garlic diet? You don't lose weight, but from a distance your friends think you look thinner! (Get it, from a distance, because you smell like garlic!)

SCIENCE SAYS...

"People who are able to laugh—
rather than being embarrassed
or angry in certain situations—
tend to have fewer heart attacks
and better blood pressure."

—**Robert R. Provine, PhD.**
Laughter: A Scientific Investigation

45 APPLES AREN'T ORANGES

- Do you measure your life against others?

- What are the dangers of comparing yourself to others?

Comparison is the death of joy.

—Mark Twain

No matter how you slice them, apples aren't oranges. Belonging to the same food group does not make them equal, not even nutritionally. Comparing two things that are unalike is fruitless and usually more harmful than good. Yet it's a trap we all have fallen prey to. We liken ourselves to people we believe are more successful, more attractive, more talented, or more financially secure. The truth of the matter is, we are only seeing their high points and not their entire journey.

I wish I could tell you that after you work through this Prescription you will be free from the tail-chasing frenzy of comparison, but there is not a lifetime immunity against it. If you aren't mindful, it subtly creeps back into your life in the form of jealousy, frustration, and self-doubt. The best thing to do is to focus on bettering yourself and mapping your own course. Each of us has a soul purpose to fulfill. Stop comparing apples to oranges—*they aren't the same.* And stop comparing yourself to others. You are not them. YOU are unique.

There is only one You

There is no person in the entire universe who has the capacity to be you. No one! That's a big statement. Remember from the earlier Prescription on belief that your uniqueness is your superpower. Stop and take a moment to let it really soak in so you can win at being you! Say it to yourself: *You are the only you.*

What an honor. But the unfortunate reality is that the magnitude of this privilege is lost when you use someone else's yardstick to measure your life. What's most unfair is that you'll always come up short. I cannot believe I am telling you this, but in lieu of saving face, I'm hoping my faux pas helps you.

I can remember talking to my best friend, comparing my talents to Oprah's (laugh now, but it wasn't funny then). She asked, "Is this really a fair comparison? If you insist on doing so, at least use similar benchmarks—her beginnings to your beginnings, not your beginnings to her decades of experience." When you stack up inequities, it's like stacking apples against pears—they're in the same family but not the same. Yes, it's okay to be motivated by the success of others, but when inspiration turns to comparison, you are insulting yourself and feeding into the lie that you aren't enough.

Grass is only greener if you water it

The perception of the grass being greener on the other side opens the floodgates to mental anguish. It's easy to get side-tracked trying to insert yourself into someone else's life. Most of the time, comparisons are made without access to the whole story, so you wind up losing sleep over artificial turf. If you want greener grass, water what is already yours by investing and zooming in on your own goals.

Many of my undergraduate classmates were from very affluent families; my beginnings were much humbler. I'll never forget a late-night discussion where, to my surprise, I learned some of them were envious of me. My mother often visited to bring some of the comforts of home—and some unsolicited guidance. Little did I know, they were jealous of my relationship with my mother. I would never have thought that I—someone who came from close to nothing financially—had something they envied, but there I was: comparing my lifestyle to theirs while they were contrasting their family dynamics to mine. Comparison achieves nothing other than, perhaps, a broken spirit.

Game over

Comparing yourself to others dims your spark. You're an original—do *not* waste time trying to be a carbon copy and letting others drive your behavior. Here are a few tips that have helped me end the comparison game—other than knowing it's a game I could never win:

1. *Only compete with yourself.* Even that's questionable, since your circumstances, resources, and knowledge are constantly changing. Of course, if you knew then what you know now, your past self might have made different decisions. But, as Jordan Peterson so fittingly phrased it, it's much fairer to "compare yourself to who you were yesterday, not to who someone else is today."

2. *Live from a place of abundance instead of lack.* We all have something to contribute to the world. I recently watched a baking competition where a competitor went to a struggling competitor's station to lend a hand. I was taken aback by his abundance mindset. He saw beyond the competition to a place where there would be plenty of space for everyone. There's room for your talents too!

3. *Know, appreciate, and showcase what makes you uniquely you.* If we were all identical, imagine how

boring the world would be. Being different is a beautiful, inspiring gift. Do not ditch your niche because it is not as shiny as someone else's. You should know what I am going to write: Everything that glitters ain't gold. And even so, silver and bronze are winners too.

4. *Celebrate and learn from others*. Offer a compliment. Someone else's win is not a loss for you. Being sincerely happy for others is a neutralizer that'll keep you from becoming green with envy.

Comparison keeps you looking over your shoulder instead of getting behind yourself and thoroughly living your life.

Don't be afraid
to be different,
be afraid
to be the same
as everyone

else.

—**Unknown**

PRESCRIPTION

For Remembering that Apples Aren't Oranges

What does it cost you when you compare yourself to others? In terms of your self-worth, self-esteem, and self-identity, it can precipitate emotional fragility. There's little, if any, upside to it. So let's take action to put an end to the comparison game—you're bigger than that.

Write a personal declaration. Each time you catch yourself comparing yourself to others, say it aloud. Try reading this one now, then get started on your own:

"STOP IT. Comparing myself to others is a needless distraction. I (insert your name) am a unique and beautiful person who was born to dwell in a space that no other person can occupy.

I have free choice. I CHOOSE to be dedicated to my own calling and send good vibes to support others in reaching their success.

I have the power to thrive in any circumstance. I will not succumb to setbacks but embrace resilience.

My narrative is right for me, and it changes as I change and my needs change. I will not focus on what others do.

My talents and gifts are impressive. I will not belittle or devalue them by weighing them against another's—I celebrate being different.

My voice and experiences are one of a kind. I will not be intimidated or envious of other people but be genuinely grateful to learn from them and to give credit where credit is due. I'm too big a gift to the world to waste my time comparing apples to oranges. I will take pride in my special qualities and cherish my ability to leave my distinct footprints in the sand."

It's time to celebrate!

You're doing so well. Look how far you've come! Your circle of friends and family are absolutely blessed to have you in their lives. I know this because anyone who chooses to take on the challenge of bringing out the best version of themselves is a real gem. On Week 45, how are you feeling about your progress? If you aren't where you thought you would be, cut yourself some slack—you'll get there.

46

KEEP LIFE SIMPLE

- Is your life running you ragged?

- What can you live without that's taking up your time?

 Life is really simple, but we insist
on making it complicated.

—Confucius

Piling up excess things in your life or having so much on your plate that you can't complete a whole task or thought has become the popular trend, the "in thing." After all, if you have lots of stuff to do, you must be important, right? The short answer is no. Busyness can be used as an escape from following through on the life that brings you the most pleasure—one that accommodates you. In truth, the minimalist lifestyle may be better suited to you. What's all the extra clutter about anyway? Less may be the more you have been searching for all along.

We've all worked long hours, taken on too many roles, and spent too little time enjoying what matters. I remember once driving from the office begrudging an evening of board meetings and other professional engagements. I thought, and perhaps even said aloud, *I just want to go home.* And for a moment, I couldn't recall how my schedule had become so full that it prevented me from doing so. In addition to my private medical practice, holding offices on community boards, chairing committees, and facilitating projects had crowded me out of my own life. Without realizing it, I had become unavailable to the most important person in my life—myself.

It's okay to say no

My intentions were good. I wanted to network, serve others, and be an upstanding leader of the community. With good intentions, I said *yes* to many things. But good intentions are not always good for us. This is a lesson I confronted over and over before I finally got it. It's not about being good at multitasking and being present everywhere except in your own life. It is about really living and noticing what adds value to your life. Honestly, some of my most rewarding times were when my schedule was completely open to welcome each moment simply as it came—no agenda. Have you experienced that too?

What is a simple life?

We cannot make more time; we have a fixed amount each day, so we have to make good use of the time that's available. We are all *too* familiar with the feeling of there never being enough time, partly because we have too much junk to do—and partly because we've complicated life by having too much junk to do. Why make things complicated when they can be simple?

A simple life means something different to each of us, but there are some common threads: It should feel healthier, happier, calmer, and freer. A blog title summed it up for me, *Living a Life Less Ordinary.* Less rushed. Less pressure. Less excess. Less overcommitting. Less agonizing. Living a life where there is time to go to the farmers' market, meditate, meet a friend for coffee, visit with family, enjoy hobbies. Once we stop being preoccupied with "more," we can appreciate the inherent gift in "less."

Make room for you

If you want to get clearer about whether something is worth your time and energy, simply ask: *Does it kindle joy?* The answer requires you to know what really matters in your life. Do you know them? Write them down, keep them visible, and add or delete as your heart's desires change.

A simpler life does not mean an insignificant life or feeling deprived. You aren't opting to do nothing while life passes you by. Quite the opposite; a simple life makes room for your passion and purpose—and for you. Paring down your life welcomes you back into it. What could be more significant than that?

Stop and smell the rain

One morning, I was running into the gym to get out of the rain. Suddenly, I stood motionless. As I stood there, my senses were amplified by the rain. I saw the raindrops as they collectively fell from the sky. I felt the dampness of the rain against my skin. I heard the gentle pitter-patter. I tasted its purity. I breathed in the fresh dewy smell. Until then, I'd always rushed out of the wet weather, but for the first time, in that moment, I really *experienced* it. Since that day, when it rains my senses are whisked back to that moment and I get out the goulashes to once again experience pleasure in something simple. I encourage you to keep your life simple enough to enjoy life's simple treasures. Maybe go for a walk in the rain?

Because the soul
and schedule
don't follow
the same

rules.

—**Emily P. Freeman**

PRESCRIPTION

For Keeping Life Simple

Less is more! Keeping life simple made my trip to Paris unforgettable. Even though it was my first time traveling to France, I decided beforehand that it was okay if I didn't visit every tourist attraction. Instead, I people-watched in Montmarte, practiced my broken French, and had conversations with natives in local restaurants. Years after the trip, I still communicate with some of the people I met. I experienced the character, charm, and spirit of Paris, which could've easily been overlooked in the hurriedness to visit every tourist attraction.

In theory, a simple life sounds well and good, but how do you actually live a simpler life? The key is to self-edit, which means removing anything from your home or environment, life, and schedule that moves you away from the life you want to live. Here's a list to help you get started.

Create a top 10 list of what matters most to you, and on a scale of 1 to 5—5 being the highest—rank the value each brings to your life.

1. Start with the items you ranked as a 5. What are the barriers that prevent you from regularly doing the things you have identified as being important to you?

2. Why are you having a difficult time eliminating the barriers in your response to question 1?

3. Set a date within the next two weeks, choose one or two (keep it simple) of the items you ranked a 5 on your top 10 list, and devise a plan to alleviate obstacles and have more free time to do them.

4. You knew this word would eventually come up: *Downsize*. Write out the sacrifices you're willing to make in order to simplify your life.

5. Over the next 6 to 12 months, work on successfully implementing these changes. For example, a smaller home, a more practical car, a different job, unplugging more from technology, less shopping.

Slowly getting back to the basics is the key to not being pulled in every direction except the one you *want* to go in. A simple life is a beautiful life.

47 CELEBRATE THE EVERYDAY YOU, EVERY DAY

- Do you celebrate yourself for what you accomplish every day?

- How do you acknowledge your daily achievements?

> In order to keep yourself motivated, and most importantly happy, you need to celebrate yourself on a daily basis.
>
> **—Dr. Nisha Khanna**

We're great at zooming in on what's wrong in our lives, but how often do we celebrate what's going well? I'm talking about the basic everyday stuff that keeps life afloat; those things are worth celebrating too!

Unless it's the high points of life, such as buying a new home, graduating, getting a promotion, or retiring, we rarely celebrate ourselves or even acknowledge the importance of our day-to-day accomplishments. Who said getting the kids off to school, picking up groceries, maintaining the household, taking care of your personal needs, and performing with excellence on the job—all while checking off the ever-growing to-do list—aren't daily victories? They are, but they usually get lost in the shuffle when it comes to reasons to celebrate. These seemingly ordinary tasks merit a "hip hip hooray," some balloons, or at least slowing down to put up your feet.

Pause long enough to honor the little things as credible moments that deserve a pat on the back for getting them done. In fact, pat yourself on the back right now and say, out loud, "Good job, Me!"

Practice positive responses to everyday life
How different could life be if you acknowledged your everyday achievements and applauded them? I'm certain you would live more joyfully and enthusiastically!

So why limit celebrations to holidays and big events when the special occasion is *every* day? Choosing to celebrate life regularly associates positive emotions with your day-to-day successes and reinforces self-gratification. Give yourself three cheers for a job well done each and every day, even when you don't feel it!

Create your own cycle of pleasure

When you create your own cycle of pleasure—purposely acknowledging and appreciating all the elbow grease and mental energy it takes to make your world go around—it changes your outlook and gives you a reason to smile. It's a big deal; don't shrug it off. Instead, enjoy a boost of blissfulness and inspiration, day in and day out, from looking forward to the simple things, the small stuff, the less glamorous victories. The trick is, the more you celebrate, the more reasons you'll have to celebrate on a daily basis.

An air high five!

What are the simple or small things? Each day, find a magical moment to give yourself an air high five! You didn't hit the snooze button, you cleared out the emails, prepared a delicious and healthy meal, made it to fitness class, finished the laundry, said no when you meant no, decided to be the bigger person, paid it forward, protected family time, kept your faith, and on and on. The magic happens every day in some way or another; seek and you shall find your reason to celebrate. Put a colorful party horn on your desk or a few pieces of confetti in your pocket as a tip to take a bow every now and then.

When I noticed all the little things I do daily that clear the path and lay the foundation for the big things, I finally got it!

The big things are all the little things strung together. To truly appreciate the big successes, I had to celebrate the little ones that made the big ones possible.

Celebrate with intention

For staying fit, I reward myself with consistent workouts. For writing this book, I celebrated each chapter I completed (52 small triumphs and rewards, any reason to buy candles). For living more spiritually aware, I wake up a little earlier to pray and meditate. Appreciate the journey. Don't save all the excitement for the final destination.

You do dozens of valuable things every day that are worthy of mini-celebrations. It could be a fist bump or simply yelling out "Yes." Although all your "awes" won't be celebrated with a cake, a gift, or a champagne toast, it doesn't make these milestones any less impactful. Embrace the idea of making a big thing about the small things. Regular self-celebrations ignite the feel-good factor that motivates you to keep pushing. After all, if it is no big deal to you, it won't be one to anyone else, either.

Every day, pause, breathe, appreciate, and feel gratitude for your small-but-mighty wins!

Don't save something
for a special occasion.
Every day of your life
is a special

occasion.

—**Thomas Monson**

PRESCRIPTION

For Celebrating the Everyday You, Every Day

When was the last time you celebrated yourself for micro-victories? You don't have to wait until you cross the finish line of the marathon; you can enjoy success as you run past each mile marker. Conditioning yourself to be festive is a big part of living a happier life. When you get into a celebratory mood every day, you create a joyful momentum in your life. Plus, you validate that good things are happening.

Make it a habit—before your feet hit the floor, before you lift your head from the pillow—to think about how you might celebrate yourself. Who says you can't recognize your daily unsung achievements? You took the stairs instead of the elevator. *Yippee!*

Now it's your turn to come up with some. Write down 10 ways you can celebrate the everyday you, every day. Build on your list as new and fun ideas come to mind. To get your thoughts flowing, here are a few ways I take pride in my miniature feats and make every day my personal holiday:

1. Dance around the house singing out of tune
2. Buy myself a new candle or essential oil
3. Slow down my pace and do nothing
4. Do something I've been wanting to do
5. Pick up some balloons or flowers to change the energy of the room
6. FaceTime with my nieces and nephews (always a natural boost of serotonin)
7. Take a walk outside
8. Watch a movie
9. Journal about my successes so I can track the progress
10. Eat ice cream (but not too often)

Your small wins may not change the world, but celebrating them can change *your* world!

48

LIVE YOUR VALUES

- When is the last time you thought seriously about what you value?

- Is your life out of step with your values?

It's not hard to make
decisions when you know
what your values are.

—**Roy Disney**

It took me by surprise when someone dear to my heart characterized her life much like that of Julia Roberts in *Eat, Pray, Love*: "You know what I felt this morning? Nothing. No passion, no spark, no faith, no heat, no nothing!" My friend was swimming against the current of her values—the compass that directs your path and moves you forward. Her choices weren't being driven by her own moral conscience. She was just going with the flow, even if the flow was drifting her away from her "true north," her most deeply held values.

We've all been there—the place where we lose sight of our own set of principles, the place where the soul doesn't feel nourished, the place where life loses direction and meaning. We've all been at the place where we are not living according to our values. The trick is to recognize when it's happening so you can get back on track.

Values anchor you to your soul

It feels like an earthquake directly under your feet, as though life is pulling you in opposition to your will. When your core values are no longer in play, life feels wrong. Something is missing. Something is out of sorts. There is a deep-seated emptiness beneath the surface of your physical being that once housed your virtues. Living apart from your values leaves nothing to anchor you—hold you securely—to your soul.

Stop hovering and land

What do you stand for? Don't answer yet. You may be tempted to rattle off something so far from your truth that it makes you cringe inside. And anyway, you cannot give an honest answer without taking a step back to take inventory of your values. If you haven't done so in a while, it's time to do so. It'll help you to keep things straight with yourself.

Knowing what's most important to you reduces your chances of wasting your time, frequenting the same life lessons, and living a life that doesn't mirror you. When you renounce values you've been accepting as your own but were really imposed on you by others, it releases you so that you can stop hovering and instead land on who you sincerely are.

Living alienated from yourself

There are two things that usually interfere with people living true to themselves. They've either never defined their values for themselves, or they go through life on autopilot, never questioning what it is they really value. Thoughtlessly falling prey to the moral ethics of culture and family can keep you alienated from yourself.

My freshmen year at the University of Michigan felt like a game of tug-of-war. I was standing in the middle of everything I had been groomed to value, yet an explosion of other students' streams of consciousness were bellowing at me. I was pulled in all directions. The time had come for me to step up to the plate and make choices about how my life would unfold—about a life that had *my* heart and soul in it. I couldn't rely on what I was told to value or what others were trying to convince me to value. I had to sit with the question *What matters most to me?* And then, answer it.

Insightful snippets you should know about values

- Values change. They are not etched in stone. Staying aware of them is a lifelong exercise.
- Values are oriented to the present moment. They determine choices you'll make right now, not next year (hopefully you didn't forget the first insight already).
- Values are only life-defining when they are lived and not merely declared.
- Values do not require validation but should be respected by others. They're not universal.
- Values should be categorized into primary versus secondary. Everything you value doesn't carry the same weight.
- Values are deliberate choices. Every decision is based on your vision for your life.
- Values are points of reference to make sure you are becoming you.
- Values evoke conscious responses, not emotional ones. Before getting into a debate, pause to remind yourself that you value peace.

Values are life's currency

A life well-lived is not lived under someone else's microscope. Aligning with your values is the currency to attract purpose, joy, fulfillment, and meaning in your life. Your moral standards—not those placed on you by others—are the medium to channel your authentic character. (Remember the "Authentic You" Prescription?) We are often under the impression that in order to come into our own we need to push harder; however, pushing deeper into the belly of our soul is what takes us closer to the source of our essence and away from pretense. We're given one life. What are you going to do to make sure it reflects who you are and what you believe? Don't be a hodgepodge of everyone else in your life.

Knowing others
is intelligence;
knowing yourself
is true wisdom.
Mastering others
is strength;
mastering yourself
is true

power.

—Lao Tzu, Tao Te Ching

PRESCRIPTION

For Living Your Values

48

It's high time you walk in your own shoes, because to know you is to love you. Just like you invest time in getting to know people you love or want to love better, spend quality time exploring who you are and what you value. Once you do, you'll never be content with being anybody but the real you. Your life won't be the same, in a positive way!

1. Make a list of values you hold near and dear (boldness, balance, connection, compassion, control, faith, fitness, wealth). Remember, no value is right or wrong, good or bad, and they can change over time.

2. Once the list is written, circle the values that speak to your spirit.

3. Create a top 10 list from the values you circled that you truly want to embody.

4. Place your top 10 list in order of importance.

5. Next to each value, write down at least two actions you can take to manifest these values in your life right now. For example, one of my values is balance. In my weekly schedule, I include activities such as Pilates, friends-and-family time, and journaling in order to bring harmony into my life.

6. Alongside each of your top 10 values, list things you are currently engaged in that compete with that specific value. Are you able to eliminate them? If not, how can they be modified so they won't be so intrusive in your life?

7. Revisit this list monthly, or at minimum quarterly, and make adjustments as you see fit. Set a reminder now, and bookmark this page.

Imagine doing what pleases you; that's living your dream!

49

GOOD THINGS COME TO THOSE WHO WAIT

- How are you patient with yourself?

- What has being impatient cost or nearly cost you?

Adopt the pace of nature:
her secret is patience.

—Ralph Waldo Emerson

I hate it when I burn my tongue on a cup of hot coffee or soup. You'd think I'd have learned by now to let them cool down. After all, they're much tastier without a scalded tongue. So why don't I wait? Perhaps I'm lacking the P gene: p-a-t-i-e-n-c-e—the ability to wait calmly. This is not to be mistaken for laziness.

Rome wasn't built in a day; man didn't land on the moon in one afternoon. They were years in the making, and no one wakes up thin after one day of a lifestyle change—I wish. Very few things are accomplished overnight; however, with time and effort your turn does happen.

Plan B or C?

While you're waiting in the wings, it can literally feel as if you're on pins and needles. Subconsciously, or maybe consciously, you start thinking of a plan B or plan C. But a standstill doesn't mean the stars won't align in your favor. It is simply taking a little longer for them to come into formation.

If it's worth having, it's worth the wait (and that's not just a cliché). In this tech-savvy world—where many things occur at a blink of an eye—that statement may be a difficult one to process; nevertheless, it's true. All good things don't happen at warp speed; some come to those who patiently wait.

Don't jump ship

Instant gratification is fantastic; but just because gratification is delayed doesn't mean it loses significance! One morning, while listening to the news, an ex–taxi driver was sharing how his impatience nearly robbed him of his true passion. After being stalled in the role of a mid-list writer, he found himself at the lowest point of his life: He and his family were homeless. That's a circumstance that would cause anyone to jump ship, and he almost did. He nearly gave up on one of the things that gave him life, his writing. Never quit what you know you were meant to do—he is now a *New York Times* best-selling author.

Funny thing, I heard his story when I was on the verge of putting this book to the side. It has been a very long time in the making, and is a true testament of my patience.

Cool, clam, and collected

Most agree that patience is a virtue, but there are other valuable payoffs for staying cool, calm, and collected. Patience lets you keep your head on straight and not make rash decisions you'll be sorry for later—boy, does that bring up memories. Science says being willing to take life as it comes, instead of rushing, is the start of something happy. Patient people report being more joyous and healthier. It also shifts your adrenaline out of overdrive and eases tension. To that point, take yourself off the clock.

Patience is life's accessory for the long journey, so pack your patience. It's a personal commitment to go the distance and get the big things done! Patience protects you from being completely wiped out by a crisis because you are able to exercise self-control. Having a little patience goes a long way, and thank goodness for that! It'll be your saving grace in your golden years. With the average life expectancy increasing, you're going to have to learn to be patient with yourself as the new, more mature you arrives.

Patience takes practice

I mentioned at the beginning of this Prescription that sometimes we're born without the P (patience) gene. If you aren't in a hurry, patience can be cultivated. Stand in a long line at the store without silently screaming *move*, or refrain from hitting the elevator button multiple times to somehow speed up closing the elevator door. Ask yourself: *What's the hurry?* In this "gotta have it right now" culture (same-day packages, information at an instant, smart carts—scan and bag as you shop), it's going to take time to rekindle the lost art of patience. And it's going to take practice:

- *Intentionally move in slow motion.* Chew your food slower. When you're not exercising, slow your walking pace. Drive the scenic route home from work.

- *Listen without any interruptions.* Pay attention to verbal and nonverbal cues: tone, pauses, posture. Then take a deep breath and count to 10—or 20—before you speak.

- *Set your own pace.* It's not about how quickly you get it done; faster isn't always the name of the game. Hop off the hamster wheel, move at your own speed, and don't be persuaded to hurry.

- *The ripple effect.* Patience won't come overnight. But the ripples from small changes that tame your impulses can spread throughout your life. When you're trying not to be sidelined by frustrations and keep at it, focus on 5, 10, or 15 minutes at a time. Little stone throws can be the build-up to mastering the art of patience.

Patience is like compound interest. Your endurance may not yield immediate gains, but over time your accumulated efforts will earn you great rewards.

Patience is nothing
more than the
willingness to live life
at the speed at which
it actually

happens.

—David Cain

PRESCRIPTION

For Good Things Come to Those Who Waits Wait

We'd all like it if things would happen at the snap of our fingers, but instead, they happen all in good time. Speed bumps have their place in your life too. Mainly, they teach you to have patience with your successes and your failures.

Let's gain a better understanding of your *im*patience so that it doesn't gain the upper hand.

1. In what area of your life is your patience being tested the most? How?

2. What are the triggers that make you feel antsy? Where is your uneasiness coming from?

3. What physical symptoms do you feel when you're impatient (i.e., irritable, not able to sleep, fidgety)?

4. How can you treat these symptoms (i.e., go for a walk, listen to a podcast, breathwork)?

5. Think of a situation when impatience got the best of you. How could exercising patience have helped you have a more positive experience?

6. This week, practice making yourself wait. Do not make any new purchases for a month, put off having dessert for a couple of hours after dinner, stick to your budget, or refrain from answering non-urgent texts or emails until the end of the day. Write down three or four ideas that will purposefully cause you to wait it out.

Keep the celebrations going!

I know this is your personal journey. But how about having a small *Celebrate You* soiree? A gathering of four to six people for the purpose of honoring and shining the light on each person's awesomeness. Everyone is the life of the party! That's one for the "Triumph" pages.

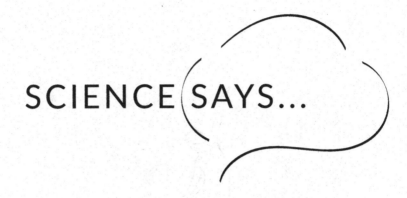

SCIENCE SAYS...

"Making yourself wait for things
that you want can not only
increase your patience,
but also make you happier
in the long run."

—A. Kumar, M. A. Killingsworth, T. Gilovich.
"Waiting for Merlot: anticipatory consumption of
experiential and material purchases,"
Psychol Sci., October 2014, 25(10):1924–31

50

DRAW THE LINE IN
THE SAND

- Have you established personal boundaries?

- Do people take advantage of your time and energy?

Daring to set boundaries is
about having the courage to love
ourselves even when we risk
disappointing others.

—Brené Brown

While I am all for not limiting ourselves, you *do* have to be able to name your limits when it comes to others, including those you love and like. There is no question that everyone needs to establish personal boundaries, but knowing what they are and setting and maintaining them is another story. Only you can and should draw a clear "line in the sand" without fear of people's reactions. If you can't, the authenticity of the relationship and what you hold as truths are in question. Even when people are fully aware of your boundaries, they will still test them. But then again, people only do what you allow them to do, right? That's right! Don't be timid. Say what you mean, and be sure to mean and *do* what you say!

Why set boundaries?

Are people trampling all over your physical, mental, and emotional space? Then it's time to set boundaries. Boundaries are extensions of your values, what matters most to you, and a tribute to your courage to honor yourself. Healthy boundaries are a reflection of intimately knowing yourself so well that you are confident about what you can and cannot do and what you want and don't want to do. They are a way to put your foot down so you can have the time and energy to embrace things that bring joy to your mind, body, and spirit. Boundaries nourish your vitality.

At some point we've all been victims of crossed lines or a lack of boundaries. I know I have. Defining personal ground rules for interacting with you isn't being disrespectful but an act of mutual respect and self-respect. It communicates with certainty how each person in the relationship should expect to be valued, appreciated, and treated. It's all well and good to be mindful of the needs of others, but not at the expense of neglecting your own. Shouldering other people's happiness isn't your job—and you shouldn't feel obligated to do it.

Setting boundaries can be a thorn in the side—if it were easy, we would all have them—so why even bother? The short answer is that people-pleasing is a hazard to *your* health, happiness, and sanity.

1. Boundaries take your life off hold.
2. Boundaries are a show of maturity.
3. Boundaries keep out trespassers.
4. Boundaries allow you to consciously stop watering down your needs.
5. Boundaries build your self-worth.

You can't be and do all things for all people. The sooner you make that clear—to yourself and to others—the sooner you can quit living in someone else's shadow.

A hard "no" or a soft "maybe"

Communication, communication, communication. You are not doing anyone any favors by having vague limits. If you're anything like me, there have been times when you said one thing and modeled another, all in the name of being a nice person. But it's rather confusing—not to mention frustrating—for everyone. You are keeping them guessing whether you are giving them a hard *no* or a soft *maybe*, which opens the door for testing your boundaries. Don't expect people to accept *no* for an answer until you firmly but politely lay down the law about what works best for you—what you need, what you want, and what's nonnegotiable from yourself and others.

Spell out the consequences

Spell out the consequences. I wish I could tell you that all you have to do is draw a line in the sand and no one will cross it. One of the hardest parts about setting boundaries is maintaining them. Inevitably, there is pushback. When most of us have thought twice about pushing limits, it hinged on the consequences.

What happens if boundaries are crossed? A word of advice: Make sure you are able to consistently follow through; if not, your boundaries won't be taken seriously by anyone, including you. Along the same lines, make sure the consequences have impact—grab the person's attention and cause hesitation. The intention is not to be unkind but to establish rules so you don't disappoint yourself while trying not to disappoint others.

I cannot give you the
formula for success,
but I can give you the
formula for failure—
which is: Trying
to please

everybody.

—Herbert B. Swope

PRESCRIPTION

For Drawing the Line in the Sand

Now that we are in agreement that life flows so much better when we set boundaries, let's take this moment to start putting up the "do not cross" tape. By the way, boundaries change periodically, so you'll need to check to make sure the ones you have established still work for you.

Before you can guard your time and energy, there must be some soul-searching in order to know and understand your limits and craft boundaries to help you take charge of your life. Up for the challenge? I'm right here supporting you. Go slow and build—Rome wasn't built in a day, right?

1. Finish the following sentences with your top five responses for each one.
   - Healthy boundaries will _____.
   - People may not_____.
   - Red flags that my boundaries are being crossed is when I feel_____.
   - I will limit my time and energy by_____.
   - When I do not feel supported or heard, I will stick up for myself by_____.
   - To protect my boundaries, I am willing to_____.

2. To avoid an unhealthy fallout, what area in your life do you most need to draw some lines in the sand?

3. How would setting boundaries in this area be instrumental in reducing stress, shielding your time, or decreasing financial burdens?

4. Your spiritual, personal, and emotional space isn't a free-for-all. Name a limit you will put in place in each of these realms that would make room for a better personal life.

5. How will you maintain these limits, and what are the consequences for violating them?

6. Be ready to talk about your boundaries, because the time will come. Write down three phrases that will help you have a conversation about them. For example: It is best for me to_____. I am not comfortable with_____. I feel taken advantage of when_____.

THE SCIENTIST SAYS...

"In work or in our personal relationships, poor boundaries lead to resentment, anger, and burnout."

—**Dana Nelson, PhD.**
Self-Care 101: Setting Healthy Boundaries, 2016

51

PASSIONATELY LIVING YOUR PURPOSE

- Are you on *your* life's mission?

- What do you daydream about doing?

Everyone has been made
for some particular work,
and the desire for that work
has been put in every heart.

—Jalaluddin Rumi

When you're on *your* mission, your purpose will make itself known beyond a shadow of a doubt, and from that moment on you'll feel safe to stop dipping your toes into life and jump all in with your whole heart.

There's something soul-stirring about doing exactly what you were meant to do. For once, nothing is missing. Contentment, abundance, and lightheartedness become the crux of your being. It's a sign that you're somewhere in the vicinity of your purpose. In the same vein, when you haven't quite discovered your passion, you often think: *Will this void ever be filled?* Don't lose sleep. Take deep breaths, and let each breath draw you closer to determining why you are here.

Believe it or not, there is something for you to do in a way that only you can. It would be a shame *not* to figure it out; you will.

Go back to your childhood

- What have you always been drawn toward?
- What makes you sparkle on the inside?
- Where does your green thumb stand out the most?

As children, we were naturally in touch with our inner self and uninhibited by external persuasions, so if you think about the things you enjoyed as a child, it can clue you in to your purpose. Even way back then, when you were a child, you had the seeds to fulfill your life's work. If you haven't already, plant them in quality soil, nurture them, and give them the proper light—attention—to grow.

Discover, embrace, and share

Discovering, embracing, and sharing what you bring to the table is one of the most worthwhile things you will ever do! When you do, you won't be able to contain your joy, no matter how hard you try. There will be a magnetic attraction to your enthusiasm and liveliness.

A word to the wise: The way you deliver your purpose to the world will continuously expand and evolve as you do. Using myself as an example, my purpose is to educate, support, and inspire people to take actionable steps to receive healing and curate health and happiness in their lives. There're many ways I orchestrate this—as a medical doctor, a speaker, a wellness expert, and an author—but they all work together to fulfill my purpose.

Your organic purpose

Are you ready to spend the rest of your life doing what you organically have a soft spot for? Yes, oh yes!

Purpose ignites passion; without it your life's flame can only flicker but cannot burn strongly. I don't mean feeling hot and heavy about everything you do. It can be as simple as the indescribable emotion you have when you're in a room full of like-minded people, feeding the homeless, working with teenagers, sitting with the elderly, creating your YouTube channel, traveling, painting, dancing, or writing your book—passion is your soul telling you that you have tapped into your calling!

I urge you not to cheat yourself. Life is much too short to waste even a second of it not passionately living your purpose.

Purpose is the reason
for the journey.
Passion is the fire
that lights the

way.

—**Unknown**

sal

PRESCRIPTION

For Passionately Living Your Purpose

What is your heart begging you to do? Find ways to express your passion and purpose in each day. Be eager to deposit everything within you out into the universe. *Give your all.* When you do, you will absolutely, positively fulfill your purpose. Let's draw up or, in this case write out, your purpose. It will be your blueprint to reassure that indeed you found your calling.

1. *P—past.* You were born for this purpose. If you reflect on your past, things should click. Life has prepared you for a time when you're unreservedly doing what you were actually meant to do. What things were you drawn to as a child? What are your hobbies and interests? Can

you see how even your personality and challenges have put you on track for your purpose?

2. *U—uplift.* It's not just about you. Your purpose should raise your spirits and those of your community. In fact, it is what binds you together because it creates a sense of belonging to something outside yourself. Your purpose is the positive impression you leave behind, and you get to feel great about it! It is a selfless, not selfish, act. What do you do that touches the lives of other people in a small or big way?

3. *R—rely.* Trust yourself. We've all been guilty of trusting other people's intuition at the expense of our own. But when it comes to your purpose, your instincts aren't wrong. It is what makes your heart throb that counts. Even if it feels out of reach, seems minuscule, or sounds ridiculous, get out of your head and go with your sixth sense. What's been hanging out in the back of your head but you keep shying away from? What have you always wanted to try but have been hesitant to step out and do?

4. *P—passion.* What makes you want to rise and shine? You've had a goose bump or two because you were excited to *get* to do it. It's simply your pleasure. It doesn't feel like work or a responsibility; you enjoy it. What are five things you unconditionally love to do? What's the common denominator? Are they all related to teaching, music, writing, healing, or helping people,

for example? The link between them is a big piece of the puzzle in understanding your purpose.

5. *O—organic.* It feels natural! It doesn't take massive effort on your part. You could almost do it in your sleep (not that you should). What are three things that come relatively easy to you?

6. *S—spiritual.* You don't have to fake it anymore. At last, your physical and spiritual persons are in harmony, and it's all because you are living your truth. Your purpose is a marriage between the values you hold dearly and what makes you feel excited about life. What three values are very important to you? What gives you genuine fulfillment?

7. *E—excellence.* You put your own spin on it. There's no doubt it's *your* signature work. It's the special way you close your podcast, the way you tie the ribbons on the boxes, the way you capture a photo, so it tells a story rather than just be a pretty picture. It's a unique twist that can't be duplicated. And people expect it from you. What is it that you do where your excellence shines through?

Time to celebrate!

This Prescription was no walk in the park. Celebrate any strides you have made toward the discovery or rediscovery of your passion. Draw a picture that reflects how you're feeling about this accomplishment.

52

INSPIRE, MOTIVATE, AND ENCOURAGE

- Where are you on your journey to healing, health, and happiness?

- What habits have you formed that'll let you build your best life?

Some days there won't be a song in
your heart. Sing anyway.

—Emory Austin

Do you feel the love? That's me sending you loads of *healthy inspiration* to stay on your journey to healing, health, and happiness. You have the power—and Prescriptions—to make your life happen! You're the ticket to your best life. Don't let fear stop you in midleap of faith. Finish the jump, and land on the absolute best version of you!

No watered-down version

The watered-down version of you just won't do. You (and no one else) will never know the difference you are supposed to make in the world if you play small to fit in and to protect yourself from life's scrapes, scratches, and bruises. They will heal.

Stop fiddling with the dimmers, and turn your light on. Live to your fullest potential, because nothing less will do. Are you *inspired?* Yes!

An open heart

As you aim to put your best foot forward in life, your whole heart has to be in it. Beating with love. Relieving with forgiveness. Filling with joy. Pumping with gratitude. Ticking with laughter. Thumping with kindness. Relaxing with patience. Flowing with peace. You won't be able to half-heartedly go after your most amazing and truest self. But when you commit from your soul and give it everything you got, your beautiful and fulfilling life will show up! Are you *motivated?* Yes!

Dr. Bernadette's basic "Bs" to live life in harmony

I don't want a meaningful and happy existence—said no one ever! It's just that sometimes we settle because it is easier, or at least seems easier. There is no sure-fire formula. It's something you will work on until you are pushing up daises—so get comfortable. That said, here's a peek at my cheatsheet for living life in harmony. It should look very familiar.

- *Become you.* You're the only one who can.
- *Begin, now.* Stop waiting to be ready.
- *Balance (I mean harmony, but I needed a word that started with the letter B).* Find the sweet spot between work and life.
- *Boundaries.* Use your time and energy to do more of what fulfills you and less of what doesn't.
- *Breathe often.* This is the most powerful and simple tool to reshape your life.
- *Believe.* If you don't, nobody else will.
- *Build strong spiritual and personal relationships.* You are not an island unto yourself.
- *Be proactive.* Take care of your health instead of being reactive about illness.
- *Be present.* Forgive, and let bygones be bygones.
- *Broaden your thinking.* Embrace new hope and possibilities.

Are you *encouraged*? Yes!

What's next?

You tell me. Why do you keep getting up in the morning? That's as good a place as any to start. After our time together, I hope one thing is clear . . . it's your choice. The world really is your canvas, and you are the artist. *Inspired, motivated, and encouraged to grab life by the horns and live your best life? Yes!*

I am grateful that you welcomed me on your journey. I wish you healing, health, and happiness.

You only live once,
but if you do it right,
once is

enough.

—Joe Lewis

PRESCRIPTION

For Inspiration, Motivation, and Encouragement

Whew, you did it! Don't you dare be modest. It took some grit and grind. But look at you now! Words cannot express how proud I am of you. Yes, you. It has nothing to do with how successful you think you were in piloting through this book. It has *everything* to do with you having the courage to want something more for your life and to move out of your comfort zone to get it. Listen; if there are some or a lot of Prescriptions you need to revisit, it's okay. As I implied in the beginning, this is personal, and it may take a once- or twice-over before you experience a shift.

And now, here's my last assignment for you: Write the new narrative for your life. This is going to take a bit of time. I don't expect you to accomplish it all in one sitting, but if you do, great! The idea is to reflect on the previous 51 Prescriptions and come up with your exclusive blueprint.

My first thought was to leave you with a blank page. Instead, I'll give you a nudge, but you don't have to be directed by this prompt—the training wheels are off. It's just here so that we end on a high note!

Journal about the reasons you *can* live your dream life and what you *can* do to achieve it. And then, with everything that is within you, go after it!

THE END or **THE BEGINNING?** It's *your* choice.

Your life is the story
that only you have the
permission to

—Dr. Bernadette Anderson

YOUR TRIUMPHS

DOODLES

ACKNOWLEDGMENTS

To my tribe, my team . . .

Saying thank you feels like much too small a phrase to express my irrepressible sentiments. There is absolutely no way I could have written this book without the abundance of support you all gave me—it simply would not have happened. The partially crafted manuscript was stored out of sight a time or two, but never out of mind. Something kept tugging at my soul. I couldn't rest knowing it was unfinished. And even with all the starts and stops, you all stayed on the journey with me. It was your commitment that gave me the tenacity to finish this book. When I placed the period at the end of the final sentence, I felt your presence. It was as if all of you were next to me with outstretched arms, ready to take the victory lap with me. To my village: Together, we did it!

Mom, you have been my cheerleader in every season of my life. In your eyes, the only things that are impossible for me are the ones I have not dreamt about yet. I knew you would gently (including a couple of pushes) nudge me to the finish when it came to this book. You did, and I love you for it. Thank you for being my supermom—everything I need, and a lot more, in a mom.

Thaddeous and Gregory (aka, Billy), my brothers who cheered by my side as I completed this book. Thaddeous, you have always expressed how proud you are of me—the feeling is mutual. I am so blessed to have you in my corner. And to Billy, who passed away not long after I finished this book ... you are always close to my heart. I am so grateful for having so many wonderful memories with you—I know you are shining your love down on me.

Dr. Jenean White, it would take me writing a book, another one, to even begin to tell you what a gift you are to me. You have literally and figuratively held my hand on this project— and squeezed it when I tried to pull away. No matter what it took, you were willing to contribute. I am beyond grateful to have you as my sister-friend forever. Girl, we have a book tour to do!

Dr. Howard Murad, you are such an inspiration to me. I owe a lot to you for your encouragement and advice, especially for believing in me and reminding me to celebrate the two-year-old in me.

Dr. Kristine Siefert, when I met you as an undergraduate at the University of Michigan, I had no idea of the tremendous influence you would have on my life. Because of you, I could—and I *did*.

Ammie Elliott, to say you are my editor is an understatement. You stepped up in every capacity that was in your wheelhouse. And you made it your priority to make me shine. Undoubtably, without you I would still be writing this book. I am very thankful to have had access to your amazing talents and skill sets. I couldn't have asked for anyone better.

Stephanie Matthews, from my photographer to creative director to friend, you have filled many roles. Since our first meeting, you were all-hands-on-deck. You not only saw the vision and believed in the vision, *you* were all aboard to bring it to fruition. You were my godsend.

Dr. Kimberly Carter, there is no other accountability partner like you. The weekly check-ins (sometimes daily ones) were invaluable in keeping me on track and putting my ideas into something concrete: a book. Each time we brainstormed, it was just what I needed.

Dr. Dorothy Jones, you have been on "Team Bernie" from the very beginning. Keep the prayers coming; they are being answered. Your unwavering endorsement is a rare gem. But more than anything, thank you for always understanding.

Pastor Timothy Clarke, thank you for your covering and praying for my strength and success.

Aubrey Rowe, thank you to my precious niece for the laugh breaks and the dinosaur hunts.

And the list goes on: Olivia Bell, Brandy Jones, Tony Jones, Michele Allen, Aunt Ethel, Aunt Mima, Ms. Cherry, Ashley Price, Kimberly King, Valerie Schick, other family and friends (you know who you are), Woodhall Press, and Salt n' Sass Writers. There are no words to express my sincere appreciation to all of you.

God, I saved the best for last. What an assignment you gave me! *"Finish the book, Bernadette,"* I heard you say over and over again. Thank you for trusting me to share these Prescriptions with the world. I feel so special to have been chosen as the author.

—Dr. Bernadette Anderson

ABOUT THE AUTHOR

Fulfilled. 52 Prescriptions for Healing, Health, and Happiness may live in the genre of self-help; however, in many ways, it is my autobiography. These Prescriptions are a part of my story—the part that let me breathe again.

I am a family doctor with 20-plus years of experience. Much to my surprise, by now I thought I would have a Hollywood star for my roles on the big screen. But, just like that star, it is easy to admire my successes without clearly seeing all of me. It is the me behind the white lab coat who empathizes with your hurts, pain, and disappointments.

I have long wrestled with unforgiveness. And loss. My dad died before I worked through my resentment toward him. I compromised my health not wanting to deal with what was really weighing me down. The scale flashed more than 300 pounds while I attempted to soothe my stress with food. I delayed my happiness to make those closest to me happy. I'll save that example for the book. I grieved in silence out of shame. No husband. No kids. I hadn't chosen not to have a family, not on purpose. I felt stuck because I was afraid to make a different choice. It was hard to admit to anyone, let alone myself, that I had devoted years in pursuit of a dream I was no longer passionate about. So you see, this book has been doctor-tested by me.

Fulfilled. 52 Prescriptions for Healing, Health, and Happiness is personal, and it is a playback of conversations with patients in pursuit of their best lives. I observed them struggle with how to get there. This book is a guide. It is my inside story and life's experiences written as Prescriptions. They are prescribed to heal the shattered pieces of the heart, to nurture a healthy mind and body, and for you to be unapologetically committed to your own happiness. How fulfilling!

BEYOND THE BOOK

Podcast & Meditation Series

In her podcast, Dr. B prescribes a method or way to achieve harmony of mind, body, soul.

Wellness Retreats

Join Dr. B and health experts in luxurious settings for a hands-on experience of the Dr. B brand and to glean simple strategies to make it a part of an everyday lifestyle.

Health Conferences

Three- and five-day collaborations with like-minded brands and strategic partners to introduce the audience to the Dr. B brand lifestyle Prescriptions to live healthier and happier.

Corporate Wellness and C-suite Retreats

Dr. B will discuss how to integrate wellness initiatives in the office setting and within the company's structure to improve the overall physical, mental, and spiritual fitness of the organization. Company leaders make a big impact on the business's culture. Dr. B's C-suite retreats can ensure it is a healthy and harmonious one.

Public Speaking, Radio Spots, and Television Appearances
Appearances and opportunities to connect with Dr. B as a thought leader, visionary, and expert.

Bulk Book Purchases
Quantity book discounts are available to your company, educational institution, or organization for reselling, educational purposes, subscription incentives, gifts, or fundraiser campaigns. For more information, email 52Prescriptions@gmail.com.

Social Media
Dr. B is a content queen! Find her inspirational and motivational posts and videos on Instagram @DrBernadetteMD, on Facebook @Life in Harmony, and on YouTube @DrBernadetteMD.